# Contents

*Figures 1–6*
These are Crown copyright and are reproduced with the
permission of the Controller of Her Majesty's Stationery Office.

# Foreword

This book is a further revision of a text which my late colleague and friend Ron Denerley and I wrote in the latter part of the 1960s when we were both consultants with the MSL Group. Reflecting the time at which it was written it was sub-titled 'in a full-employment economy'. Much has happened in the employment scene since that time: full employment has given way to large-scale unemployment almost overnight and we are told that it is likely to remain above the 5 per cent level for the forseeable future; a major change in taking place in attitude between employee and employer; further research has been done and subsequently attitudes changed towards certain selection techniques. These changes have been reflected in this new text. Of course many practices and procedures have remained more or less constant, and no change has been made for its own sake. Every effort has been made to ensure that the text is up to date, down to earth and readable.

From the first an unorthodox approach has been used throughout this book. A deliberate attempt has been made to provoke constructive re-thinking about current recruitment and selection practices. The aim has been to make the book of day to day value to personnel specialists and to line managers to help them to cope better with the varied recruitment problems they meet in their work.

Some frequently recurring recruitment situations have been depicted through the eyes of would-be candidates. This form of insight is an extremely valuable one and needs to be cultivated by anyone who tries to understand the attitudes of candidates which is such an essential part of the assessment process. These case-studies (pp 67–103) have been called *Reflections on recruitment* and draw attention to mistakes which are commonly made. No apology is offered for the criticisms made, as indeed criticism is the proper starting point if standards are to be raised. However experienced you are in personnel selection, it is hoped that these will encourage you to look again at the way in which recruitment is actually being carried out in your own organization.

In choosing case study material, a wide range of jobs have been portrayed. This is to emphasize that 'good practice' must

5

necessarily vary according to the type of job being filled. Most previous books on recruitment seem to have overlooked this fact, or it has not arisen, as they have essentially been written for one segment only of the market. A good deal of space has been devoted to the specific aspects of attracting a strong field of suitable candidates. It often seems to be forgotten that no amount of interviewing, however skilled, can ever produce high-calibre employees out of indifferent applicants. This point, too, has been neglected by previous authors.

Since this publication has been conceived as a practical guide, only oblique reference is made to the many researches which have been conducted into many aspects of the total recruitment and selection process; while the scientific approach to selection techniques has been closely considered they have been kept in perspective. Readers with a thirst for research should find consolation in the Bibliography.

A note of caution should be addressed to students and to others entering the personnel field for the first time. Over the years I have helped to teach and to coach many students from a wide variety of backgrounds in the art and skill of recruitment and selection. I have also run courses for experienced executives who have had great difficulty in finding suitable jobs. Truly horrifying tales have been recounted during these courses of inadequate selection procedures and of grossly inhuman treatment of candidates. Much of this arises from thoughtlessness and from the belief that only a little basic knowledge is needed to become a first class selector. This is not so. Some of the major pitfalls are pointed out throughout this text, but the uninitiated should not regard the book in any way as a complete 'do it yourself' kit. Reading it will not by itself make anyone proficient at recruitment any more than you can learn to play a violin or drive a car simply from a text. Sympathetic training, ruthless self-criticism and the attempt always to look at the process through the eyes of the candidate are, in my experience, the only satisfactory ways really to improve one's performance and skill.

Finally, I would like to record my gratitude to Ron Denerley and another former colleague Dominic McDonnell for their help with the original edition much of which still forms the hard core of this text. I am also grateful to many former students, colleagues and clients whose helpful criticism of the original text and ruthless questioning of established practice has frequently brought me up short and forced me once again to get my perspectives and values right. Once again this text has been revised to reflect the economic revolution which is taking place in the industrialized world. The apparent decline in the traditional heavy industries, the rise in high technology, the implication of the use of computers, the leisure-related industries, the changing status of women in western society, awareness of the need to accommodate ethnic minorities; all of these trends are going to have a profound effect on working practices and the lives of the vast majority who want to work for a living. The implications of these changes can only be lightly touched on in this short text in so far as they are already having an impact on current recruitment and selection practice but their longer term implications are as yet far from clear. No doubt this text will soon be overtaken by events but the principles will probably remain largely intact and readers will be able to make most of the necessary adjustments without too much difficulty.

PRP
1985

# Perspective

## i  The nature of recruitment

People make companies. So, in a real sense, do all those involved in the recruitment process.

Human beings are the life-blood of any enterprise. They are, literally, a company's most vital assets. The profitability—and even the survival—of an enterprise usually depends upon the calibre of its workforce. Since the recruitment process either opens the company's door to prospective employees (or slams it in their faces) the proficiency with which it is conducted is of crucial importance. Recruitment is not only concerned with engaging a required number of people: it is also concerned with measuring their quality. It is not only a matter of satisfying a company's present needs; it is an activity which influences the shape of the company's future. Its cumulative results predetermine the future health of the enterprise.

It is sometimes argued that recruitment constitutes the most important single aspect of the personnel function. Be that as it may, the costs of inefficient recruitment are formidable in financial expenditure alone; the indirect consequences are more difficult to quantify, but are probably even more costly in human as well as in financial terms.

Efficient recruitment and placement procedures are a prerequisite to the development of an effective workforce. A person placed in unsuitable work is either unable to reach the required standard of performance or is working under physical or psychological strain. If those stresses do not actually cause him or her to give up the job, they are likely to give rise sooner or later to frequent absence, ill health, breaches of discipline or conflict with fellow employees. Whether the employee resigns, is dismissed or struggles on, the result is costly in economic and human terms. Moreover, in many cases, an employee who leaves after a week or two and is regarded as 'unsuitable', might have been more efficient and content to stay if placed in a different kind of job.

In recent years it has become increasingly appreciated that recruitment is a two-way process. Initially this was forced on employers by the acute shortage of a skilled and experienced labour force, and more recently through a major change in attitudes towards work. Few people today will accept unquestioningly dull, meaningless tasks. Thanks to the welfare state they can (just) afford to wait. This has had a profound effect on attitudes to work and life; people want to lead meaningful lives, to have time to enjoy leisure and a share of the good things of life. Thus at a time of high unemployment people are reluctant to move house; they want to be able to discuss jobs and terms and are not prepared to be pushed about or become slaves of their employers. Jobs have to be sold, terms negotiated and a much more flexible approach adopted by employers. Recruitment, especially recruitment at higher levels, is no longer a question of trying to fill a closely defined slot but rather an attempt to match the needs of the organization with the skills and aspirations of the individual applicant in an optimal way. There are several side benefits. Having thus had a major say in the selection process, the individual is perhaps better motivated to perform well in the new job; but perhaps more important the process of self-selection is encouraged which research tells us is a valuable and reliable counter-check to our own assessments.

One of the effects of joining the European Economic Community has been the adoption of 'best practice' in many aspects of employment by the various member companies. The Employment Protection Act has introduced Belgian-style security of employment for the individual. It is now difficult to fire an unwanted employee, and it can be very expensive. A judgement of 'unfair dismissal' can lead to heavy fines, compensation payment and reinstatement of the unwanted employee. Discrimination can be held to exist at any point in the selection procedure—and the employer brought before an industrial tribunal for public examination. This is placing an increasing responsibility on the shoulders of the recruitment and selection specialists. They must ensure that their company attracts and retains the best people available in each category. They must also build a long-term human resource which is adaptive, flexible and does not become so over-specialized in any segment that redundancy must inevitably arise.

An important aim, then, in selecting new employees should be to ensure that, as far as possible, they are placed in jobs where they have a strong expectation of being well-adjusted to their work and to their environment. The effectiveness of the recruitment methods

in any organization must be judged by the degree to which this aim
is achieved in practice. It must be remembered that there are social
and moral implications to recruitment work, as well as the obvious
economic aspects. Recruiters, through their power to offer or
withhold employment, are instrumental in changing the course of
people's working lives. The commercial doctrine of *caveat emptor* is
a feeble line of defence if applied to the employment situation. The
personnel manager is better placed than the prospective employee
to see both sides of the fence and to anticipate the consequences of
inviting the individual to give up one job in order to accept another.
Redundant executives can find themselves in acute difficulties if
they make unwise moves after a steady career, and can risk being
turned from highly sought-after recruits to 'failed executives' in a
short space of time. The onus is on the employer to act responsibly.
There are inescapable social obligations which cannot be shrugged
aside.

## ii Employment in the 1980s

If we look back over the last 65 years employment falls into three
distinct periods with a watershed during the second world war and
again in the 1970s. The 1920s and 1930s saw massive unemployment; the 1950s to 1960s full to over-full employment; the 1970s
the start of a new era as fundamental as the industrial revolution.
There have been violent swings between sudden and large-scale
unemployment, including a new phenomenon—that of executive
redundancy—followed by an unprecedented scramble for certain
categories of labour. Undoubtedly at first redundancy became a
socially acceptable means of getting rid of unwanted labour, and
many inadequate performers swelled the ranks of the unemployed.
But mergers, take-overs, reorganizations, violent contractions
in certain industries and the persistent introduction of new
technology is taking its toll, placing many excellent people
suddenly on the market place through no fault of their own. Many
have remained there for years largely because they have been
encouraged by their companies to become so specialized that they
are an 'unwanted commodity' and one which is too expensive and
perhaps unwilling to be retrained. As little as ten years ago
employees who changed their jobs after three to five years were

often branded as unstable: today the employee who stays in one job with one company for from five to ten years is regarded as unambitious and potentially redundant. Before and immediately after the second world war young people were encouraged to join large organizations in the belief that the organization would look after them for life and indeed through retirement. With the collapse of such giants as Rolls Royce and the massive contraction in major companies and indeed whole industries this belief was finally shattered. Increasing attempts by successive governments to manage the economy, the 'threat' of nationalization or privatization has lead to changes in attitude towards the objectives of companies. Profit is still a 'dirty word' to all people except management—even in a 'siege economy'. Companies are expected to be socially responsible in their actions, and workforces are demanding to be consulted before a merger or a closure. Private manufacturing industry has become a high risk employment area: many nationalized industries are in disarray and government employment is only marginally more secure. Today it is expected that most employees will try to build their own careers and that this will almost certainly mean working for a number of employers; and it may also mean one or two quite major changes such as a second or even third career.

Harassed personnel selection officers scarcely know whether they are coming or going; one minute they are recruiting hard and the next minute declaring people redundant (see figure 6, p. 176). You may well question the value of sophisticated recruitment and selection techniques when many employees are only going to be needed for a relatively short time, and when those needed most can afford to call the tune anyway. This is understandable, but it must never be forgotten that a company's human resources are usually its most valuable resource. It is also an increasingly expensive resource; to attract the best available it must be used effectively and efficiently. This calls for more rather than less skill in both recruitment and selection. Hit or miss is a luxury which cannot be afforded. If few applicants reply to an advertisement, the human resources specialist will need to review the job and the terms offered and may also need to go out into the market place and seek out and persuade potential candidates to come forward. Selection may be difficult but a true assessment must of necessity be made of each applicant; positive recruitment and selection can then take place rather than the traditional whittling down of a large list of applicants by a process of elimination on a series of negative factors.

The development of modern recruitment concepts is of relatively recent origin. Progress has been accelerated partly in response to economic pressures and partly as a result of a wider understanding of psychological and sociological aspects of work. More progress is needed; there is still a great deal we do not know.

## iii The main stages of the recruitment process

The exigences of the 1939–45 war acted as a powerful spur to the development of personnel selection methods. The 'national emergency' required a mammoth redeployment of human resources. In the UK and in the United States, millions of men and women had to be absorbed quickly into the armed forces and into industries 'essential to the war effort'. This major upheaval provided the opportunity and the incentive to search, on an unprecedented scale, for more efficient methods of allocating people to jobs they would be capable of doing. Naturally, mistakes were made. But the intensive efforts of those five years produced some valuable ways of measuring human qualities and of predicting whether or not people would be likely to succeed in different jobs. Conditions were of course abnormal. Conscription was in force and people could be directed by law into essential work whether or not they wanted to go. Even so, much of the knowledge about personnel selection techniques acquired during that period has some relevance to the total selection situation. Further progress has been made since then in identifying and in measuring human attributes that correlate with success in different careers and occupations. In Britain some notable efforts have been made particularly by the former National Institute of Industrial Psychology, in applying more systematic selection techniques in the industrial environment. Perhaps inevitably, attention has continued to be focused until recently on the use of techniques for assessing people. Undoubtedly, assessment skills are an important factor in recruitment work, but the sustained publicity given to this particular aspect has sometimes tended to create an unbalanced picture of what recruitment itself is really about. Job change and a thorough understanding of the demands of a job on its incumbent is the foundation of matching the skills and attributes of individual people to it. Assessment techniques cannot produce high-calibre employees out of indifferent candidates. They can merely establish that none of those candidates should be offered the job. Unless the exercise of other skills has ensured that the field of candidates includes some with the required attributes, the job cannot be filled satisfactorily. Lest this point be dismissed as a statement of the obvious, it should be emphasized that, in practice, its implications are regularly forgotten. In Britain today, there is no conscription of labour. People are not directed compulsorily to jobs. The recruiter has the task of making them aware that a job is vacant, of arousing their interest and of stimulating them to apply. Thus, important phases of recruitment work must precede the use of assessment skills.

Recruitment is often thought of as the 'finding, assessing and engaging of new employees'. But this shorthand description is incomplete and potentially misleading. It is pointless to embark on a recruitment programme without having established, in the first place, what human qualities make for success or failure in the job to be filled. In essence, recruitment is a matching process; and the capacities and inclinations of the candidates have to be matched against the demands and rewards inherent in a given job or career pattern. From this, it follows that anyone undertaking recruitment must first acquire a clear understanding of the job to be filled; purposeful steps must then be taken to attract the interest of people possessing the attributes demanded by that job. Recruitment is better conceived as being made up of four complementary stages, each one of which is important in its own right. These stages occur in the following sequence:

1 Assessing the job
2 Attracting a field of candidates
3 Assessing the candidates
4 Placement and subsequent follow-up

These four activities have been adopted as the framework of this publication and provide its main subject matter.

By its nature, recruitment is concerned with the future. Both implicitly and explicitly, it involves making judgements and forecasts about how people will adjust to new work and how they are likely to behave next week, or next month or next year. Human predictions about the behaviour of other people are fallible and all recruiters should have the humility to admit that they will be wrong sometimes. They will be wrong less often if they adopt a systematic approach to this task than if they rely on superficial hunches. The risk of mistakes and the probable margin of error can be reduced by a systematic discipline of collecting and weighing the relevant evidence. In this way, the recruiter can also improve and learn from earlier mistakes and from those of other people. This represents a worthwhile step forward, and is as much as we can hope to achieve in the present state of knowledge. Recruitment is more an art than an exact science, but it calls for a scientific approach.

# 1
# First stage—
# establish the basic facts

"Need the job be filled at all?" is the first question which always needs answering. It is surprising how often the question is never asked—let alone answered convincingly. There appears to be a built-in reflex action which tempts many of us to assume that recruitment has to be undertaken simply because an employee is leaving. That assumption is often unjustified by the facts.

Every vacancy presents management with an opportunity and with a choice. The opportunity is freedom to consider whether the job is necessary (and, hence, a chance to re-allot the work or part of it to meet the changing needs of the organization). The choice is between recruitment and other courses of action (such as internal promotion or temporary transfer).

Before anyone can think critically in these ways about a vacancy, it is necessary to have a clear idea of the work that is presently being done and of the way it complements work being done elsewhere in the organization. We must also establish why the job exists at all, its objectives, the role the incumbent has to play. Jobs grow: there are needs, people with suitable backgrounds are recruited or transferred; the need is then fulfilled according to their own strengths and weaknesses and to their own interpretations of the roles they have to play. As years go by, the jobs grow or are redefined or split up. Jobs tend to continue with the incumbent or by tradition. The classic example of this is the spare man in the artillery team; on investigation it was discovered that he was originally there to hold the horses and the purpose of his job had been forgotten when the artillery were mechanized! One suspects that there are still many jobs of this nature in industry and commerce today. So before we assume that there is a vacancy we must establish the purpose of the job and the role the incumbent is to play. We must then attempt to measure the 'hole' so that in turn we can measure possible 'pegs' and if we can use an identical

15

measuring device, so much the better. We dignify these preliminary measurements by the title job analysis. The larger firms
employ trained job analysts who undertake occupational studies in
a highly formalized way. But even the smallest firm should apply
the elements of job analysis to all its jobs, if it is to ensure that it is
making the best use of its human resources and if it is to avoid
mistakes in making new appointments.

Much of this handbook is about the techniques of recruitment
and selection. Techniques are important. The purposes for which
they are used are even more important. It is absolutely essential to
establish, right at the outset, whether and if so why recruitment is
necessary; and there are some simple questions which should
always be considered before seeking new employees.

## i Job analysis

To analyse a job* we need an accurate description of the work
actually done and an understanding of this work in its relation to
jobs done elsewhere in the organization.

The description of the job should be based on evidence
collected from various sources:

(a) obtain a verbal description of the purpose of the job and its
    position in the organization from a person directly in charge of
    the work (supervisor, head of department or director concerned)
(b) observe the job being done (and, in some cases, try it out to
    distinguish learners' difficulties)
(c) discuss the work with one or two people doing it and identify
    the tasks performed, guidance needed, proportion of time
    spent on various tasks, difficulties encountered, etc
(d) study personnel documents which may reveal aspects of the job
    neglected in practice.

The resultant description may be broken down into the following
five areas:

---

*The word *job* is commonly used in many senses so a few definitions are necessary:
*Job* – a collection of tasks which constitute the work of one person
*Task* – a major element of work intended to achieve a specific result
*Occupation* – all jobs sufficiently similar with regard to their main tasks to enable them to be
grouped together

*The purpose of the job*—this sets out in one or two sentences the organizational objectives of this particular appointment.

*Position in the organization*—this should show to whom the incumbent should report, it should identify the department and division and, if there are both line and staff reporting relationships, these should be briefly explained or indicated on a simplified organization chart.

*Principal duties and responsibilities*—a list of the key tasks the incumbent will have to perform should then follow; it should also indicate limits of authority and where applicable other people or departments who must be consulted. These are the parameters of the job, stated succinctly.

*Specific tasks*—here the job description may go into more detail, setting out what specific tasks must be done and the way in which they should be done. We may do this by reference to other publications such as an operating manual or management memoranda or departmental instructions. However, this should be done sparingly as specific tasks may be short-lived and may give rise to avoidable disputes when a manager wishes to make even minor adjustments. (It should be remembered that, strictly speaking, a new contract of employment should be drawn up and agreed every time a job specification is materially changed).

*Working relationships*—this should set out briefly other positions, departments or organizations the incumbent must deal with in the performance of the job. This may include organizations outside the company such as government departments, customers or suppliers.
The 'understanding' of the job demands an interpretation of: *organizational factors*—how the job relates to other jobs in the department and to similar jobs elsewhere in the organization—how the organization is developing and how the various departments, occupations, jobs and tasks contribute to its total work and objectives. In a period of very rapid technical change the division of work within any organization is constantly changing as one task becomes obsolete and a new one is added to cope with new equipment and new activities. This argues the need for *regular* job analysis.

*personal factors*—the level of knowledge, skill, experience needed to perform the job satisfactorily; the physical and social environment in which the job is done; the opportunities for promotion or transfer; the pay, benefits and less tangible rewards associated with the job; the temperamental demands of the work, etc. The 'personal' interpretation of the work to be done provides much of the material for building the Person Specification which is a basic tool of recruitment and is described later in this chapter.

Given an accurate description of the job and an interpretation of the organizational and personal factors which affect its performance, we possess the basic data required for any recruitment work. Such basic data produced by systematic job analysis can, moreover, form a factual background for dealing with other facets of personnel management, such as:

*training*—the content of training courses can be planned to provide the precise degree of skills and knowledge required in the work.

*human resource utilization*—jobs can be structured to accommodate special skills which are available or to make the most economical use of scarce talent; jobs may be combined, enlarged, divided, used for training, or adapted to suit the skills of otherwise redundant employees elsewhere in the organization. Jobs can also be abolished.

*salary and wage structures*—traditionally depend upon accurate ranking and evaluation of jobs within the organization.

*joint consultation and negotiations*—proceed more smoothly when facts are available.

The job analysis should always be checked for accuracy and completeness with the head of the department concerned, before it is put to work in any of these ways. The checking process itself often sparks off minor organizational changes and re-allocation of duties. This process of change is continuous and even the most thorough job analysis may be a little out of date in some respects within a short time of its completion.

Whether job analysis is conducted by a full-time specialist working with splendid forms or by a hard-pressed 'generalist' using plain paper and native wit, it remains an essential preliminary to all that follows in this handbook.

There is no easy short cut to job analysis. Four sentences on a sheet of paper coupled with a few hieroglyphics are not adequate either to the selector or to the new incumbent. An old job description may be worse than useless. Management consultants largely thrive because companies fail to carry out this stage of the recruitment process thoroughly and satisfactorily. It is a sheer waste of time and extremely hazardous for all concerned to attempt to recruit without a clear picture recorded in writing of the job to be done and the context within which it must be performed. Acceptable standards of performance should in some cases be spelled out as well. Where possible, factual data should be given as this avoids misunderstandings later. It is also useful to the selector for later evaluation and 'evolution' of success or failure.

## ii The person specification

Job analysis yields the basic material needed on which to compose a person specification. Given a clear idea of the work to be done, the circumstances in which it will be carried out and the levels of performance demanded, it is relatively easy to determine the level of skill and knowledge required and the amount of experience needed for a successful performance. The total specification—that is the specific job description plus the broad generalized description often never recorded by in-company personnel of the company outlook and management style tell of the social and economic influences that will bear on the worker, and thus of the personality attributes that the successful applicant should possess. Mentally, we are already beginning to match an ideal person to the job. It is often useful at this preliminary stage to think of individuals we have known, and as it were to try this specification out on them. The tendency is always to draw up an over-idealized specification. Matching this specification in our mind's eye with the actual people we have known helps us to keep our feet on the ground and to distinguish the really essential from the ideal. If we are seeking to replace someone who has held down a job for a number of years, it is pointless drawing up a specification which accurately portrays the person concerned minus all blemishes but with all the necessary in-company knowledge: this will almost certainly be an impossible specification against which we can recruit. We must get right down to the absolute essentials and think in terms of what the newcomer to the department or company must have if he or she is to perform this task satisfactorily. The more flexible the person specification, the more flexible the recruiter can be at the later stages of negotiation.

Moreover, today the recruiter must ensure that no inexcusable discrimination is explicit or implied in the person specification. If a non-indigenous person is to be excluded there must be concrete reasons, and 'balance of the races' or 'personal preference' is not acceptable. Many managers still find it hard to accept this and raise artificial criteria in the hope that this will exclude the undesirable. Indeed, the law in its attempt to be just leans the other way. (Incidentally, for appointments abroad this restriction may not apply). The same is true with the artificial allocation of jobs between men and women. It is only the exceptional job that cannot be performed by both sexes—not the other way round (at the time of writing a woman has successfully fought for a place in a professional football team and a man has insisted on being considered on his merits for employment as a chambermaid— accepting the condition that he will need to share a flat with a female, but not the bedroom!)

It is important that the person specification be drawn up not in terms of abstract human qualities but in terms that may be recognized and measured objectively so far as possible.

The late Professor Alec Rodger sounded a warning on this point some years ago: "If matching is to be done satisfactorily, the requirements of an occupation (or job) must be described in the same terms as the attributes of the people who are being considered for it". He might have added that it is not helpful to ask for attributes that cannot be assessed by the selector or the selection process.

The two classifications of human attributes in most common use for selection purposes are Rodger's own seven-point plan and the five-point plan popularized by T Munro Fraser:

| *Seven-point plan* | *Five-point plan* |
|---|---|
| Physical make-up | Impact on other people |
| Attainments | Qualifications |
| General intelligence | Brains and abilities |
| Specialized aptitudes | Motivation |
| Interests | Adjustment |
| Disposition | |
| Circumstances | |

Many readers will be accustomed to summing up individuals under one or other of these schemes. But the real purpose and subtlety of these 'plans' is that they enable both jobs and people to be quantified and measured with the same yardstick, so that simply matching point by point can result in good results and managers can be dissuaded from becoming amateur psychologists. In preparing the specification it is important to consider under each of the above headings:

*Essential attributes*—those which are indispensable if the job is to be performed to satisfactory standards.

*Desirable attributes*—the less essential characteristics which may be little more than preferences.

*Contra-indications*—attributes which would disqualify an individual or group of individuals even though all other criteria are favourable.

Essential attributes and contra-indications should not be too readily specified. The task of recruiting a suitable person can be made impossible if too rare a combination of attributes is demanded. In listing 'desirable' qualities, guidance should be provided for the selector by indicating the amount of latitude which can be exercised in various directions: for example, by defining alternative types of experience that could be considered if the preferred type *is not available.*

Precise language is taken for granted when an engineering specification is being drafted. It is no less important in a person specification. Thus, a 'good' education, 'average' intelligence, and 'acceptable' appearance are descriptions that will be interpreted very differently by different people. Education can be defined in terms of academic achievement (but beware the relative levels of the various examinations and grading systems used). 'Acceptability' should be defined in terms of the person or people who must accept the candidate in the performance of the job. Similarly, abstract nouns should be avoided in preparing the specification (and also the job specification). Vague phrases such as 'responsible for inspection of output' leave too much room for possible misunderstanding. Whenever possible, activity words and quantitative dimensions should be used—for example 'inspects' followed by a definition of which products, how often and to what tolerance standards, and reference should be made to other documents in which agreed standards of performance have been defined, eg sales contracts, BSI, MOD standards etc.

The person specification should be completed by considering information about types of people who have been successful or unsuccessful in the job. Such information is usually available in every personnel department and is obtained through exit and grievance interviews, through hearsay, or by examination of statistical trends.

### iii Questions to ask before recruiting

*What is the purpose of the job? Is it necessary? Is it fulfilling its purpose?*
— The job analysis reviewed and brought up to date will answer these questions.

*Could it be combined with another job or jobs, or could tasks be re-allocated to make better use of other people in the department?*
— If the job requires special skills and experience which exist but are not fully employed elsewhere in the organization, re-allocation of work is often the fastest and least costly solution.

*Can we learn any lessons from the record of the last incumbent?*
— The findings of the exit interview and the regular performance appraisals by the department head may confirm or contradict what has been recorded in the job analysis and in the person specification. Particular attention should be given to the leaver's comments on the most difficult aspects of the job, since these often reveal unsuspected tensions and pressures within the department.

*Could the vacancy be used as a temporary training position, eg the youth training scheme; or to accommodate an employee redundant elsewhere; or to provide easier work for an employee approaching retirement or in failing health; or as an opportunity for promoting someone?*

— A study of the person specification will often suggest possibilities for transfer, training or promotion.

*Are we certain that no existing employee would be suitable? Could we afford to train someone?*

— The recruitment and selection of specialized experience from outside the company is often a time-consuming, expensive and uncertain business. The retraining of an existing employee may be expensive too, but can be a reliable way of overcoming the scarcity of specialists, usually generates goodwill and may be partly offset by a training grant.

*Is the required type of person easy to recruit locally? Are there aspects of the job analysis (eg hours of work) or of the person specification which could be adjusted in order to attract a wider choice of candidates?*

— The removal of an unpopular or inconvenient element from a job may ease the recruitment situation. (For example, introducing special evening shifts may make it possible to recruit part-timers or older people.)

## iv A note on human resource planning

*Longer term measurements*

The cost of staff has risen relentlessly over the years. Even at times of high unemployment we are experiencing national shortages of many types of skilled and unskilled people. Because of these shortages recruitment costs have risen and some recruitment exercises produce poor results. There are companies which have had to abandon or postpone new development plans because of staff (and even management) shortages. Little wonder that governments and industry today take into account the availability and needs of people in their economic planning and budgeting.

In its simplest form, a human resource plan takes account of the main staffing changes that can be expected over a number of years and it outlines the provisions that must be made for recruitment, training and transfers. Naturally, the complexity of such a plan will depend on the size, complexity and facilities of the organization it covers. There used to be a national manpower model. Many of the managerially more sophisticated companies use computerized personnel records and advanced mathematical techniques to forecast their staff intake over the next decade. The 'do it yourself' personnel manager in the small company falls back on the wit and plain paper used for job analysis. Thought processes parallel the work done by the computers elsewhere; the principles are unaffected by the size of the problem.

The main elements in human resource planning are summarized below.

*Stocktaking:* the present position must be known before we can begin to analyse changes expected in the workforce. Tables showing the age distribution, the patterns of skills and experience, the organization structure and the wage and salary levels are prepared and superimposed. We should know the labour turnover figures and trends for each occupational group and the training time for new entrants to every job. One of these variables or any group of them may drastically affect the total picture. Evidently, computers have their uses with so many variables. But much progress can be made with bar diagrams and annotated organization charts.

*Movements:* retirements are fairly simple to predict. Resignations less easy, unless labour turnover has been studied for some years. Transfers and promotions are often a consequence of new business developments (see below). The supply of trainees and the fall-out during and after training must be predicted.

*Policies, organizational and technical changes:* if the manpower planner's work is to be complete, it is vital that he or she has access to the company's overall plans for growth (or contraction) to interpret these in human terms. Diversification policies, a decision to alter marketing methods, expansion of research, the introduction of mini-computers to the offices—changes like these will substantially alter the human resource plan. Attention must also be given to changes in occupational content that may follow the introduction of new techniques (eg many fitting and inspection jobs have been de-skilled by the introduction of transfer machinery, and the training time for such work is consequently shortened). The 1980s is seeing massive changes in management style, organizational structures and skills requirements calling for accurate assessments of individuals rather than simply categories of staff.

*Legal requirements:* the implications of any new laws on employment must be considered and allowed for. Equal opportunity could mean higher labour turnover or more flexibility—and inevitably will mean higher labour costs. The change from 'commodity' to 'resource' attitudes towards the workforce, the high cost of redundancy, the need to 'cover' work for employees absent on maternity leave or to fulfil civil obligations will all affect plans. Many employers are experimenting with the use of temporary labour and there is a rapid rise among the self employed and in home 'networking', using developments in computer technology.

*Determining future needs*
From the forecasts of the scale and shape of the future organization, the human resource planner deduces the numbers and types of people it will require. This is not entirely a crystal ball exercise. Even if a major change in production policy has been forecast, it is still possible to determine likely labour content by skills and numbers.

Forecast requirements for each new occupational type are then compared with existing 'stocks' and adjustments made for losses through retirements, resignations, promotions and transfers. It should not be overlooked that an unbalanced age or salary structure may suddenly accelerate losses. Forward adjustments are made for *entrants* who may come from training schemes, transfers or promotions.

The difference between forecast requirements and the adjusted 'stock' figures provides an estimate of the recruitment and training needs over the period being reviewed, and can be built into an annual budget constructed on a departmental or occupational basis. In deciding how many people to take on yearly, further adjustments must be made to allow for the known levels of wastage during training and for losses at the end of training as well as for change in the development or contraction of the enterprise.

In reaching decisions on recruitment and labour policy

towards the end of a human resource planning exercise, it is
realistic to ask
— what proportion of our needs can we (or should we) try to
     recruit from outside sources?
— what proportion should we attempt to train ourselves, using
     present or improved training resources?
— what internal movements by promotion, job rotation,
     transfer, retraining, re-allocation of tasks do we wish to
     encourage or discourage?
— what likely redundancies have we uncovered and what is to
     be done about them?

Human resource planning is complicated especially at a time
of economic uncertainty, but it is better to attempt to plan than to
leave things to chance. Most of the required information should
already be available in the personnel department, but its true
significance begins to emerge only as the plan is constructed. A
human resource plan is necessarily based on a snapshot of the
organization at a particular point in time. Many factors will occur
inside and outside the company which will necessitate the updating
of this plan at regular intervals. A quarterly revision for the short
term coupled with an adjustment to the longer term plans will be
sufficient. But the longer term must not be neglected as many
training schemes take many years to complete and, at the
apprentice level, it may be five years before the new recruit
is effectively contributing to the company's labour force. If
depending heavily on local colleges it also helps them to plan future
facilities and courses.

## v Steps in analysing a job—an example

1  The personnel manager is notified that the records clerk in the
   drawing office (DO) has handed in her notice because she is
   leaving the district.

2  He arranges to discuss the job with:
   the drawing office manager
   the woman's section leader
   the woman herself.

3    The manager can only spare five minutes. She says the clerk is a pleasant woman and she is sorry to see her go. She hopes the replacement will be a stayer because it is important to have continuity on records. She thinks everything has gone smoothly lately on records but is not in touch with the details of the job.

4    The section leader provides an abundance of comment and information. He lists the records maintained by the clerk, who runs a type of library system for recording details of many thousands of drawings and issuing and retrieving prints. He estimates the number of drawings issued daily; the enquiries received by telephone, the time spent on searching the files and records. He takes the personnel manager to watch the woman at work with her cabinets and telephone at the end of the DO. She is carefully entering identification details from a batch of new drawings on to pre-printed record cards. As she works, she is interrupted three times by telephone enquiries about tooling and pattern numbers. These she answers by referring to a mini-computer on her desk. One of the draughtsmen comes to her desk with a query. She answers him and then they chat casually for some minutes. She continues to enter details on her machine while talking. The personnel manager examines some of the entries she has made on the cards, notes the complexity of the computerized records, notes also the height and extent of the suspension files which occupy one wall of the DO and notes the calm and concentration of the clerk.

5    Later, the personnel manager sees the records clerk privately to discuss her reasons for leaving and to learn more about the job, her attitude to it and her attitude to the company. He asks her what parts of the job she found difficult to learn, what she will be most glad to get away from when she leaves. He gets examples of the sorts of question she receives by telephone and finds that she uses her memory a good deal, has devised a way of classifying some types of information regularly needed by adding extra signals to the computer records, and prepares a monthly print out for the cost accountant listing all tools reported broken or re-ordered. (This was not mentioned by the section leader.) He then goes on to talk about the district she is moving to. He gains the impression that she has enjoyed her

work which has brought her into contact with many departments and that she is sorry to be leaving.

6   There are no records in the personnel department about this job. It appears to have grown up around the woman who was recruited four and a half years ago as a school-leaver. Initially employed on tracing (she had done mechanical drawing at school and had asked for training as a draughtswoman), she was given responsibility for records when they were reorganized two years ago.

7   The personnel manager drafts a job description, carries out his job analysis and then prepares a person specification. These drafts may be modified in a final talk with the section leader and drawing office manager, and will then serve as the yardstick by which he will seek and assess candidates for the job.

## Job description

*Title* Records Clerk
*Department* Drawing Office
*Accountable to* Section Leader (Designs)
*Supporting staff* None
*Number employed on this work* 1
*Replacement available* None
*Position from which candidates for this position might come* DO trainees
*Avenues of promotion/transfer from this position* Higher grade clerical work

1   *Purpose and objects of work*
    Ensures that all drawings and prints in current use can be identified and located, that only up to date drawings are in use; that dimensions of tools and patterns in use can be checked centrally; that records are kept of tool breakages for costing purposes.

2   *Activities*
    (a) Issues classification numbers for all new drawings and enters details on to mini-computer records.
    (b) Enters dates and modification details to records when drawings are modified. Destroys all unmodified prints.

   (c) Files drawings and spare prints in appropriate lateral files.

   (d) Maintains register of re-ordered tools and prepares monthly summary for the cost office.

   (e) Answers queries from production departments, DO staff, cost office, relating to modifications in progress, tool and pattern identification numbers, location of prints.

   (f) Requisitions new prints and issues prints to works departments noting dates and quantities issued.

   (g) Regularly reviews files for obsolete records. Informs section leader when additional filing capacity is required.

3  *Circumstances*

   (a) Work subject to continuous interruption by telephone and by personal enquirers.

   (b) Due to growth of business, volume of work increasing monthly. Two new suspension filing cabinets added recently.

   (c) Estimated number of queries per day: 50

     New drawings registered daily: 15 (average)

     Drawings issued daily: variable. Builds up to peaks when new lines are being introduced.

   (d) Most time spent satisfying queries. These often involve searching records and telephoning other departments.

   (e) Main difficulty is concentration in spite of interruptions. Work demands accuracy, a liking for routine, a helpful disposition and an easy social manner.

## Job analysis

Personal requirements

   *Educational and vocational knowledge* No qualifications essential. Good school record needed as evidence of application, concentration and intelligence (see details below).

   Experience of dealing with engineering drawings and ability to distinguish main features is desirable.

   *Experience* Minimum age about 18. Prior experience of record keeping essential. Previous experience of working with computers would be valuable. Ideal experience would be in a production scheduling or sales administration office of an engineering works, or as a trainee in a drawing office for at least a year after leaving school.

*Physical effort and skill* Some reaching into tall cabinets. Minimum height about 1m 60. Work is mainly sedentary.

*Adaptability and concentration* Routine work, subject to interruptions, requiring close concentration.

*Intelligence* No complex problems to solve. Above average intelligence would be unsuitable.

*Disposition and temperament* Critical requirements are a helpful, patient disposition and a liking for routine work involving accuracy. Must not be shy. A friendly and brisk manner is appropriate.

Responsibilities

*Controls* no staff. Takes no decisions affecting others.

*Contacts* are informal and with drawing office personnel, supervisors and departmental heads. No external contacts.

*Confidential information* as for all DO staff.

*Assets and materials* Responsible for care and safe custody of essential records.

Special features

*Working conditions* Pleasant newly-built office. Brisk and friendly atmosphere.

*Difficulties* Growing volume of work and enquiries.

*Consequence of error* Inaccuracies and omissions by the record clerk could result in delays to manufacture or even manufacture of obsolete parts.

*Supervision received* Main check is absence of complaints. No direct supervision possible because of degree of detail.

*Satisfaction* In solving queries and providing an efficient service—in range of contacts within the company.

*Conditions of service* Weekly staff terms. Job graded as C with merit increments. Current salary £xx at age 20.

## The person specification

*Physical make-up*       Minimum height 1m 60
                            Pleasant appearance
                            Brisk, clear speech, free from inpediments

| | |
|---|---|
| *Attainments* | Essential to have evidence of application, concentration and capacity for detailed work |
| | Desirable to have some knowledge of technical drawing and of engineering terms |
| | Education should reflect academic or technical drawing and of engineering terms. Education should reflect academic or technical bias. Four O levels or the Previous experience of record keeping in technical office or library is essential |
| | Experience of working with engineering drawings is desirable |
| *General intelligence* | Brisk reactions and an accurate memory are needed rather than ability to solve complex problems |
| *Specialized aptitudes* | Neat, quick and accurate at clerical work |
| *Interests* | Practical and social |
| *Disposition* | Self-reliant, helpful, friendly |
| *Circumstances* | A person who is likely to stay for at least three years is preferred |
| *Contra-indications* | Obvious shyness or a grasshopper mentality |
| *Possible sources* | |
| Internal — | Transfer from production, sales, planning or DO? |
| External — | PER?, YTS? Advertise? |

# 2
# Second stage—
# attract a field of candidates

## i A guide to recruitment sources

A company's ability to recruit new employees depends to a high degree upon its enterprise in making known the opportunities it has to offer. Only if someone who meets the person specification is prompted to apply can the job be filled satisfactorily. The overriding importance of this basic position must be borne in mind constantly.

Of course, interviewing and other assessment techniques also occupy an important place in recruitment work, but they can do nothing to improve the relevance or the quality of the field of candidates. No amount of interviewing will ever produce high-calibre employees out of indifferent candidates; it will merely establish that none of the applicants ought to be engaged.

It is essential, therefore, to set about the task of attracting candidates in a systematic and well-informed way. A number of judgements have to be made about the probable availability of suitable potential candidates and about the most effective and economical means of reaching them. In effect, a deliberate appraisal of the prospective candidate market must be made in order to define the catchment area and choose the most appropriate channels of communication.

An analysis of a firm's recent recruitment results and personnel records for similar jobs will quickly reveal the geographical areas which have tended to be most productive in the past and may serve as a guide to the future. For jobs at every level, the feasibility of recruiting locally should always be considered first, in view of the high costs of removal and rehousing. The boundaries of the normal catchment area for factory employees and office staff often will be determined by the public transport system. Exceptionally, a firm may penetrate more remote areas by shouldering the cost of providing special transport. Temporary pockets of labour will become available elsewhere from time to time, due to factory closures or redundancy, and the Department of Employment will give considerable assistance in tapping these. Even so, the catchment area theory will still hold good and skilled people will often transfer temporarily to semi-skilled jobs near their homes rather than face a long journey to work or a move to a different part of the country. There are still marked differences in attitudes to geographical movement in different parts of the country, or indeed overseas, exacerbated by widening differentials in the cost of housing and ease of council house exchange.

For professionally qualified staff and for managerial appointments the net often will have to be cast more widely—but not haphazardly. Some estimate should be made of roughly how many people meet the person specification, and of where they are most likely to be working at present. Only after so doing can the most appropriate channels of communication be chosen and used in a judicious way.

As a long term policy, it is sensible to maintain close personal links with local schools, colleges and employment agencies: to keep them fully informed of opportunities for employment, training and promotion: and to encourage them to visit the firm and acquire progressively a good understanding of the type of work and the working environment. In a company where morale is high, many office and factory vacancies can be filled by the simple expedient of encouraging employees to draw such vacancies to the attention of their friends and relatives; and some firms pay a bonus to employees who introduce new recruits.

External sources of candidates include Department of Employment branches, university appointments boards, local employment agencies, management consultants and the numerous journals, local radio stations and newspapers in which recruitment advertisements can be published or broadcast.

The relevance and value of such external services must vary enormously according to the type and level of the jobs to be filled. Generalizations can be wide of the mark because of fluctuations in supply and demand at different times and in different localities, but the summary below may serve as a tentative guide to the more usual sources of candidates:

(a) *School leavers* Youth Employment Service; YTS; direct links with schools; supplemented by some advertising in local newspapers and special programmes on national radio and television.

(b) *Factory staff* Mostly via Department of Employment and advertising in local newspapers; occasionally, cinema or poster advertising. For certain skilled trades, trade union officials can help or may be 'mandatory' (eg Fleet Street printers), and local radio and television advertising (including Prestel) can be an economic proposition in some areas, especially if large numbers are required.

(c) *Office staff* Employment agencies, especially for secretaries and typists; local and regional advertising; Department of Employment; local radio advertising.

(d) *Professionally qualified staff* Most professional institutions carry advertisements in their journals and/or have an appointments service for the benefit of their members; national, regional or local advertising; Professional and Executive Recruitment (operated by Department of Employment); specialist recruitment agencies.

(e) *University graduates* University appointments boards; personal links with academic staff; advertisements in careers publications, supplemented by some national press advertising if large numbers of graduates are sought.

(f) *Managers and senior technical staff* Selective advertising in national 'quality' newspapers and professional journals; management selection and executive search consultants; PER; university appointments boards (occasionally); the Officers Association; employment registers; outplacement consultants registers.

## ii Recruitment advertising

Press advertising is one of the principal means of attracting applicants. It is not the only means and other possible sources of candidates (such as those mentioned above) should be explored whenever appropriate. But since every personnel manager is likely to have to advertise some jobs at some time, the strengths and limitations of advertising as a recruitment technique merit fairly detailed consideration.

Job advertising has a long history, but more radical changes in methods—and costs—have taken place since 1958 than occurred in the whole of the previous century. This process of rapid change is likely to continue through the current decade. Advertising is now a more powerful tool of recruitment than ever before; on the other hand, if used inexpertly, it can be extremely costly as well as disappointingly unproductive. It is hardly surprising that personnel managers may sometimes feel perplexed and frustrated. This is bound to happen unless they acquire a firm grasp of certain basic principles. That is not to imply that they must master all the technical aspects of the subject, since they can rely on an advertising agency for guidance and support in such matters. But the more clearly they understand what can and what cannot be achieved by advertising, the better the results they are likely to obtain. Some observations on the services available from advertising agencies are contained in the next chapter.

The packed pages of large advertisements displayed in national and local newspapers did not exist before 1958. Until that date, import controls on newsprint had limited the size of newspapers, and traditionally job advertisements had been limited to announcements and carried in the lineage columns only: hence the amount of space allocated to classified advertising was severely restricted. All 'situations vacant' were printed in small type generally in alphabetical order, and delays of four to six weeks were common. After the removal of import restrictions, newspapers began to offer facilities to display advertisements and to catch the eye of the person who was not actively searching for a job. It would be fallacious, however, to assume that such people have either the time or inclination to read all the advertisements. But an increasing proportion of ambitious people scan these pages. This is partly because the advertisements have become much more informative; discerning newspaper readers can pick up clues about trends in salary levels and keep abreast of topical developments in their own industry or occupation. Also, today people have to think about their future prospects and to weigh these against the longer-term prospects of the company advertising. Thus, both at times when unemployment is exceptionally high or exceptionally low, advertisers can receive a poor response: it appears that people prefer to live on state assistance than to risk further redundancy and those in employment to stay put unless the new job offers an exceptional opportunity in an environment where the quality of life or educational opportunities may be higher.

But as advertising has become a more powerful tool of recruitment, the cost penalty of inefficient advertising has multiplied out of all proportion. In the 1950s three or four insertions of a 'small ad' would cost under £50 altogether. If that same job were displayed at the time of writing once only in one national newspaper the cost would exceed £2,000 for a very modest advertisement. Hit or miss methods have become a luxury in which no company can afford to indulge. Advertising calls for greater skill and precision than ever before. A firm grasp of certain basic principles is essential:

- Advertising is a means to an end and not an end in itself. Since the desired objective is efficient recruitment, advertising must be conceived as an integral part of the recruitment process. It is not a separate activity to be rushed through before the real business of selecting people begins.

- The function of an advertisement is to produce action. It is not enough for an advertisement to be seen; it must also work by conveying information which stimulates a positive response.

- The foundation of every job advertisement should be a careful analysis of the job itself.

- Every advertisement should be aimed as directly and as explicitly as possible at the type of person defined in the person specification.

- Prospective candidates are most likely to respond to an advertisement when uncertainty and latent doubts have been dispelled from their minds by telling them what they would like to know.

## (a) Aims

In planning an advertisement, the personnel manager will aim to achieve three objectives:

- to produce a compact field of candidates equipped to do the job and motivated to accept it. This implies a conscious effort to *minimize the number of unsuitable applicants.*

- to secure the optimum balance between coverage and cost in the process of communicating with an outside audience.

- to facilitate future requirement—rather than prejudice it— since all advertising has some side-effects on the advertiser's public image.

By its nature, an advertisement can convey only a snapshot impression of the complex variables which characterize a job and differentiate it from other jobs. This must be so since, even after a half-day visit to a prospective employer, a candidate takes away only a superficial impression of what it is really like to work there. How then can advertising help us to communicate effectively in the recruitment field? Some guide-lines can be found in the more intensive research which has been carried out in the field of product advertising and where the logical approach to an advertising problem is to search for answers to three fundamental questions: What to say? How to say it? Where to say it? These same questions can be used as the basic mental framework for planning recruitment advertisements. Before examining each one in turn, it should be noted that recruitment advertising differs from product advertising in several important respects:

- Product advertising is usually conceived as a planned series of advertisements based on initial market research which will take the reader through several stages, from a complete unawareness of a product through to an understanding of its special features; from advantages and disadvantages through to a readiness to buy. The recruitment advertisement, with the notable exception of large scale planned campaigns (eg for nurses, police officers, train drivers) has to do the total job in one advertisement, on one day in one publication.

● The time cycle is much shorter. Product advertising is usually planned months in advance, whereas in recruitment only one week may lapse between a vacancy arising and the finalization of the advertisement.

● The results of recruitment advertisements can be measured more accurately and more quickly. The proficient advertiser will establish within a few days whether value for money has been achieved, irrespective of whether this be £50, £500 or £5,000.

● The recruitment advertisement appears cheek by jowl usually on a double page spread in direct competition with other advertisements of the same or similar nature, whereas the product advertisement is usually of a larger size and does not have to compete directly. In many ways the recruitment advertisement is much more akin to editorial than to advertising matter. The advertiser does not attempt to pre-empt or to dominate the page in most cases as this is far too expensive, but instead has selectively to appeal to the eye and mind of the appropriate reader.

● A vast response is generally not wanted, except in special recruitment campaigns. Time and money is consumed in reading and replying to applications; and when a company needs to fill only one vacancy, the receipt of hundreds of applications is not only an embarrassment but a serious financial burden, and increases the risk of charges of discrimination since selection has often to be somewhat arbitrary in the first selection. The gross number of responses cannot, therefore, be regarded as an indication of advertising efficiency.

*(b) What to say?*
Fact-finding is an essential prerequisite to drawing up an advertisement. Unfortunately, many job advertisements tend to be written in a hurry. Sometimes an unexpected resignation has produced a crisis and a replacement has to be sought urgently. Sending an advertisement to the press does at least seem to

demonstrate that the situation is being tackled promptly and to provide a few days' breathing space during which other urgent work can be attended to. The temptation to fall into this trap is very real and must be resisted. An advertisement will only succeed if it conveys the right information to the right people who are, by definition, outside the company and who either know nothing about you or have a very distorted view based on hearsay. A careful analysis of the job itself must be the foundation of the advertisement. The mental discipline of drawing up the job and person specification will sometimes throw a new light on facts which had been overlooked or considered unimportant, but which to an outsider may be critical in determining whether to reply to the advertisement.

It is easy to underestimate the effort which has to be made and the emotional strains involved before anyone will put pen to paper and submit an application to another company. Prospective candidates are most likely to do so if they can recognize from the facts given in the advertisement that the job is one which they would like to do and which calls for their particular training and experience. Many research studies have shown categorically that what most would-be candidates look for in an advertisement is a description of the job to be done, its location, the remuneration offered and the type of person required.

The contents of the advertisement should therefore be factual, relevant and unambiguous. As far as possible, they should convey the key characteristics of the job and person specification, as well as information about the benefits and about the company. In selecting facts for inclusion in an advertisement, the personnel manager's greatest strength—possession of an intimate knowledge about the job and the company—can be her greatest handicap. She may be prone to forget that the prospective candidate does not start off with that same framework of background knowledge. The personnel manager's task is to stimulate the interest of a group of people who, by definition, cannot know all that she herself knows; and to do this she must try to put herself in the position of the prospective candidate. This means formulating hypotheses about what the candidate already knows and what else he needs to know before he will take the significant step of submitting an application. Why should such a man give up his present job in order to move to this one? What distinctive advantages do we have to offer? Are we justified in assuming—even though our products may be well-known—that the candidate really knows what it is like to work here?

Inclusion of a salary level in the advertisement often presents difficulties—but its omission can cause even greater ones. At the time of writing (1985) a fundamental change is taking place in salary levels which may be a temporary phenomenon. Salaries are being geared to the 'added value' of the individual to a particular organization rather than to traditional market rates. This is resulting in very wide differentials for what is the same job between capital intensive and labour intensive industries and beween the successful and the struggling organizations. This attitude to salaries may need to be reflected in an advertisement if one is to be competitive. Usually there is no objection to mentioning fringe benefits. What is likely to be lost by giving a quantifiable indication of salary? In larger organizations, company policy will often govern what may or may not be said in the advertisement; but, even then, it is not always clear when and why that policy came into being. Conjuring with evasive statements such as "an attractive salary will be offered to the right candidate according to qualifications and experience" is not likely to solve the problem. It is merely side-stepping the issue. The discerning reader will deduce that the company either does not know what salary it should be paying, hopes to get away with as little as it can, or would face awkward questions from its present staff if the salary level were disclosed in the advertisement. None of these interpretations helps the advertiser. Salary or remuneration package is the only universally understood yardstick for describing the rewards of the job in such a way that the potential candidates know they will not be wasting their time by applying. This is not to imply that money is the only criterion used when assessing the comparative attractions of different jobs; but a woman currently earning £25,000 pa is unlikely to accept a job offered to her at £20,000 pa; nor does the man being paid a modest £8,000 pa usually expect to be offered a job at twice his present salary. Faced with these economic realities, it is usually desirable to quote salary whenever possible; but, failing this, it is better to say nothing at all in the advertisement than to waste words—and money—on circumlocutions which convey no real meaning.

The advertisement should also enable the reader to assess

whether or not readers can see themselves in that job and to assess their chances of being offered it. This can be done by specifying the candidate's requirements in explicit terms and by distinguishing clearly between those characteristics which are deemed to be essential and those which are desirable. The advertisement can also give an outsider a feel of the company, of the environment, of the demands and of the opportunities offered. This can sometimes be done by describing the probable record of the ideal applicant, or by postulating a possible future career pattern. Tough demands are better spelled out: to the right person a difficulty represents a challenge to their expertise or scope to make an impact and gain high visibility in an organization. If, for instance, the job demands a large amount of overseas travel, the employer is interested only in receiving enquiries from people who are prepared to do this. The advertisement can therefore screen out unsuitable applicants as well as help suitable applicants to identify themselves with the job and the company. Given a reasonably accurate forecast of the size of the candidate market for a particular job, the response to an advertisement can be regulated by placing greater or less emphasis on the desirable requirements. Fashion in age parameters vary and it is likely that discrimination by age will be made illegal. Until then do not be unnecessarily restrictive—a likely age band is more realistic than a tight, arbitrary one.

A recruitment advertisement must be accurate, and not reveal any evidence of bias or discrimination. It is not sufficient to imply that the job is open to men and women: the advertisement must make this clear. The word 'manager' is said to imply 'male': even if the likelihood of finding a suitable woman is nil it must still be stated that this appointment is equally open to men and women. Wags have tried to get round this and got away with it—but beware! (Two examples come to mind: a cook was wanted 'who had been trained in Scottish cooking in the home'; an ad for navvies warned 'that applicants must be prepared to work stripped to the waist outdoors in the summer!') Your advertising agent can advise you if they think you are breaking the law. Accuracy and truthfulness are also being questioned and deliberately misleading statements—even if included as a smokescreen—could well become suspect. Remember, whilst you may be allowed to publish a loose statement, if it is subsequently challenged, the onus will be on *you* and not on the publication or the agent.

The best way to avoid possible discrimination will probably be to write longer, more definitive ads so that candidates can match themselves more accurately to the salary offered, length and depth of experience being key 'exclusion factors'.

People engaged in the recruitment activity must never forget that the sum of the parts may result in an unsaleable proposition. A job advertisement must represent a viable proposition if it is to work. In other words person specifications and job descriptions cannot be drawn up in isolation from the market place. The job, the person specification and the remuneration package must be such as to appeal to a certain band of people who exist and who can be attracted to this proposition. This may sound obvious but many employers become so inward looking and out of touch with current movements in the market place that they waste time and money on an ill-conceived recruitment campaign. The executive searcher tries to visualize the prospective candidate at work—by industry, geographical location, down to specific 'target companies' and jobs. A quick survey of the market place by sounding-out people at the right level soon reveals whether or not the job is a saleable proposition. If not, it is wiser to review the basis and thinking behind the proposal from first principles.

### (c) How to say it

The aim must be to present an attractive and concise pen picture in terms which will be interesting and familiar to the people who the advertisement is designed to attract. This requires a knowledge of the candidate market and a knowledge of people and the things that matter to them in their work. The advertisement must appeal not only to those on the job market but also to people who are already employed, and to whom it will offer a vision of greater job satisfaction. No one applies for another job unless there is likely to be some personal benefit by so doing. The art of writing an advertisement, therefore, lies in identifying the features of the job situation which will have positive appeal to the targeted candidate and in conveying them accurately and convincingly.

The heading of the advertisement is of paramount import-ance. Detailed information given in the text will never be read at all, unless the heading has first caught the attention of the desired audience. The parallel between editorial and recruitment advertising is particularly apt here. Headline and opening paragraph should contain the excitement of the job. They are both factual and emotive and must induce those candidates you particularly wish to attract to read further. The heading does not necessarily have to be the job title, although very often it is. Job titles can be notoriously vague or misleading. The title industrial engineer may be applied in one company to a job which has little in common with the job of an industrial engineer in another. A development engineer may not even bother to read an advertisement headed principal scientific officer if he is unfamiliar with this kind of grading. The title—and the whole advertisement—must be attractive when seen through the eyes of the candidate. The words of Robert Burns are worth reading in this context:

> O wad some Pow'r the giftie gie us
> To see oursels as others see us!
> It wad frae mony a blunder free us,
> and foolish notion.

Unfortunately, the wording of an advertisement is often determined by what is acceptable to, say, the works director because the vacancy is in her department, even though the works director's liking or otherwise for the draft may be of little relevance. The advertisement has to attract people who may be of an entirely different age group, background and outlook. The advertisement must be written for and speak the language of the desired applicant; whether it appeals to you or me or to the works director is quite irrelevant. It is always worth obtaining a critical second opinion on the draft of a proposed advertisement; often this can be provided more usefully by someone who is at the level of the job that is to be advertised.

The sequence of the text should be arranged so that priority is given to information which will hold the reader's interest. The wording needs to be checked for its relevance and brevity. If it is too long, interest may be lost. When appealing to candidates in other parts of the country, it is worth indicating that assistance with housing and/or removal expenses can be offered, if it is the company's policy to provide such assistance. Particular attention should be given to the way in which the candidate requirements are expressed. Is the phrasing too exacting or too loose to achieve the appropriate degree of self-selection and self-elimination? And, if the reader does decide to apply, will the text give him or her positive guidance on how to do so?

The majority of advertisements will carry the company's name and address with an instruction that applications should be addressed to the personnel manager. Inclusion of the telephone number will increase an advertisement's pulling-power but the administrative implications must be considered. There is no point in inviting people to telephone unless someone will be available to talk sensibly to them. The layout should be designed to catch the eye of the casual reader who is merely glancing at the page. Large black areas can command attention, but the subtle use of white space gives visual distinction to an advertisement and also ensures that the heading is read. Illustrations or graphics will add character to an advertisement, but they must be chosen carefully to appeal to the right audience. On the whole gimmicks should be avoided. Research has shown that people take themselves seriously; when they are considering changing a job the vast majority of people dislike gimmicks. Illustrations, if included, must say something positively, in their own right, and can usefully convey far better than words the fact that you want young lively people to apply; or they can give information such as a picture of a new product or appeal to the imagination by a sketch of a foreign country. Such illustrations must be appropriate and well drawn or they will detract from the message the advertisement is attempting to convey.

Experience shows that advertisements must be kept short and to the point. The so-called *Daily Mirror* rules apply—sentences should be short; 15 words perhaps being the ideal; there should be plenty of paragraphs; one sentence, one thought; stick to basic English; say what you mean and avoid obscure terms; 150 to 200 words is ample for most advertisements. Much can be conveyed in a few words if we consider the advertisement through the eyes of the candidate. Most people communicate in speech by a form of shorthand; provided that the right shorthand is used, this can work most powerfully if we use the same framework of reference of our candidates. Given the critical and relevant data, the specialist can rapidly gain a picture of the type of organization: the accountant looks for financial information; the production engineer, information on plant and systems of working and on products handled; the personnel manager is more impressed by a breakdown of numbers of people employed and the level of sophistication of personnel techniques employed. This type of shorthand speaks much more loudly and forcibly than vast quantities of irrelevant data or a sparkling description of the person desired in broad general terms without saying anything about the job to be done.

In recent years there has been an increasing tendency, particularly among the larger companies, to adopt a house style of advertisement layout in order to reinforce a corporate image. There can be worthwhile advantages in building up recognition value in this way; but such house styles must be designed so that they can be adapted flexibly to meet the different situations. Otherwise they can obscure the principal object, which is to focus attention on the job to be filled. As a general rule, people are primarily interested in the type of work rather than the identity of a particular company, and the layout of the advertisement should reflect those priorities. Advertisements in a distinctive house style may also give rise to suspicion that something is wrong with a company which always seems to be advertising for staff. Such feelings may be groundless but, if regular advertising has its roots in expansion rather than excessive labour turnover, there is much to be gained by using the fact as a positive feature of the series of advertisements.

The limitations inherent in box number advertisements are fairly severe. People who are reasonably satisfied in their present work are understandably disinclined to despatch confidential information about themselves to an anonymous recipient, when they have no means of knowing whether they would want to join (or rejoin) that company. Box number advertisements have diminished appeal in a period of full employment, and in periods of unemployment they appeal primarily one suspects to the employer who does not want to bother to reply to all the enquirers or who wishes, say, to screen out all redundant executives or exercises some other form of blatant discrimination but does not wish his name to be associated with such action. Of course there are times when the box number is correctly used; these are rare and abuse has tended to detract from their true effectiveness.

*(d) Where to say it*
Selection of the most appropriate advertising media requires knowledge of the coverage, pulling-power, cost and timing of the

medium in question. The personnel manager should keep a systematic analysis of the quality and quantity of response obtained from the publications in which previous advertisements have been placed. This will enable comparative judgements to be made about those publications which are used regularly. But, apart from local recruitment, the need to advertise one particular kind of job may arise infrequently and the personnel department will often lack up to date statistical data about the reading habits of the type of person they want to attract. It makes economic sense to ask the advice of an advertising agency rather than rely on hunch or intuition. In the absence of reliable facts, the common tendency is to play safe by using more publications than may be strictly necessary. This can be a costly practice. Taking space in one extra newspaper can add more than £2,000 to the outlay; and if this is done regularly the annual recruitment bill can be inflated by many thousands of pounds. At the other extreme, and if there is no urgency, the advertisement can be booked to appear in only one specialist trade or professional publication at a cost well below, say, £1,000, and the results awaited before deciding whether additional advertising media are needed; but if this exercise should prove to be necessary, the indirect cost of the wasted working time may outweigh the sought-for savings on advertising.

In considering which publications to use and the style of layout to be adopted it is necessary to visualize the proposed advertisement in the context of those publications and to assess its probable impact. The salient characteristics of the main categories of advertising media can be summarized as follows:

*National newspapers* theoretically ought to be the least attractive proposition on economic grounds but in practice offer the best service and often the greatest likelihood of making an early appointment, particularly for jobs at the more senior levels.

Advantages: minimum delay before publication provided that space is booked at the earliest opportunity, speed of circulation; quality of type-setting is usually good; proofs will be supplied; 'reassurance value' arising from wide circulation.

Disadvantages: comparatively expensive, with each column centimetre (a very small space) costing £40 or more at the time of writing; volume of other competing advertisements; wastage factor, since the majority of copies are sold to people who cannot be remotely suitable; brief period of exposure—though the quality Sundays usually have a shelf-life of 2–3 weeks against the 2–3 days of a daily.

*Local newspapers and free sheets* Recruiting locally avoids the risks and costs of resettlement but presupposes that a sufficient number of suitably experienced people exist within that geographical area and that they look for a change of job in the local paper.

Advantages: lower costs; can serve as a useful vehicle for public relations; little delay.

Disadvantages: unsuitable for more senior appointments; quality of typesetting may vary from good to indifferent; some do not provide proofs; many are read very selectively.

*Specialist journals* The professional journals and trade papers read by people having the desired qualifications or interests in the relevant industries ought, on the face of it, to be the most useful channel of communication. Their pulling-power for recruitment advertisements varies enormously and in many cases is disappointing.

Advantages: compact and homogeneous readership; comparatively inexpensive because of smaller circulation; readers likely to be keeping abreast of developments in their particular field.

Disadvantages: possible delays between issues; slower circulation after advertisement is published; job advertisements are tucked away at the back of some journals along with miscellaneous announcements about second-hand machinery, trade services etc.

It is unwise to make hard and fast rules about the selection of media. At the time of writing (September 1985) the cost of advertising is still rising rapidly, in spite of an unprecedented high level of sustained unemployment: serious delays in the national press due to industrial action against computer typesetting: and many otherwise disregarded media have begun to show very good returns. There is also a growing belief that certain types of individuals never read or respond to job advertisements. While this may be true of some individuals who are happy in their jobs, experience has proved time and time again that an advertisement can work at virtually any level provided that it is well worded. The advertiser has to judge not only the readership but also the job-seeking habits of the potential market; they are not static but this is difficult because the relevant data are not available. Mere readership figures do not tell you how many people actually scan the 'situations vacant' pages either regularly or occasionally. The larger recruitment agencies will tell you that readership habits can vary over a period of a few months almost without rhyme or reason. Again, an advertising agent who sees a vastly wider cross section of advertising than you will ever do yourself can give you guidance on this point.

Advertising rates depend largely on the size and composition of a publication's readership and on fluctuations in demand for advertising space. For job advertisements publishers usually quote two rates:

(a) *Lineage* 'x pence per line'. Used for small advertisements of not more than one column width and set in the standard size of type used by that publication. The personnel manager pays for the number of lines occupied by the advertisement.

*Semi-display* If you wish to have your lineage advertisement spread out a bit more with a bolder heading you can buy space in the lineage columns of say three to four column centimetres, which in theory gives you a greater impact; much depends on what other advertisers do on the same day and, as your advertisement is set by the publication, you have no control over its final appearance.

(b) *Classified display* '£y per single column cm'. The personnel manager should specify in advance the area of space to be occupied, eg '20 col cms triple column'. This would mean an area 10 centimetres deep across three columns wide—there being nine columns across the width of a typical newspaper page, and the cost would be 30 times the rate quoted per column centimetre.

A scrutiny of each publication will indicate which style is likely to be more appropriate for the level and kind of job to be advertised. Although the use of displayed layouts has grown enormously in recent years, it is still quite possible to obtain a satisfactory response to a well-written lineage advertisement for certain kinds of jobs, especially those for which the newspaper provides a ready-made and appropriate classified category. It should be noted that by accepting an advertisement the publication does not guarantee that it will appear on a particular date or occupy a predetermined position, although reasonable requests can usually be met.

*Television* Both national and regional networks will take recruitment advertising and will advise on the most suitable times. Costs vary enormously according to time of year, time of day, day of week and sometimes proximity to a major programme. Special rates are available and many of these are considerably cheaper. TV may be used in two ways: either as an advertisement in its own right or as a pointer to press advertising which appears in the next few days. TV can make a massive impact in a very short time.

Advantages: speed, penetration of the market; useful for mass recruitment, especially at operative levels.

Disadvantages: cost; a vast amount of wasted circulation can produce a massive response which is hard to deal with; very brief period of exposure (15 to 30 seconds).

*Local radio* As more and more local radio stations have been established and the quality of programmes has improved, and in response to unemployment especially among the young school leavers, many local radio stations have mounted special campaigns, sometimes free of charge to employers, to help bring together employers and job seekers—especially in the smaller companies. This has been supported on occasion by local recruitment drives with co-ordinated radio, press and poster advertising. To date, local radio has been most successful in recruiting skilled, semi-skilled, clerical and retail staff.

As much recruitment as possible should be planned well ahead, thus giving time for any relevant specialist publications to be considered. Seasonal factors should be taken into account, and the imminence of Christmas or summer holidays may influence the wording of advertisements as well as their timing. Recruitment advertising is essentially a means of communicating. It involves a series of personal judgements about the job and about the candidate market. In particular, the attitudes of potential candidates must be anticipated and understood in order to communicate with them successfully. The forces of supply and demand exert a strong influence on the candidate market and hence on the prospects of filling any particular job. It is pointless to attempt the impossible. Advertising cannot create people who do not exist; nor can it fill a job nobody wants. But when advertising judgements are based on reliable and relevant facts and when the principles of effective communication are observed, advertising serves as a powerful and penetrating tool of recruitment.

## iii The role of the external support services

Personnel management has earned recognition as a specialist branch of management only during the last half century. Not only was it a late starter compared with other functional specialisms such as the sales, production and financial aspects of management, but its structure and scope are still growing steadily. The personnel manager's role is very different today in most companies from what it was 25 years ago; and often has available a range of specialist support services which did not then exist. The nature and the acceptance of these specialist services has reflected the successive stages in the evolution of personnel management itself.

In the 1920s the main theme was welfare, and the first services which arose to support the 'labour officer' in her or his newly-formed role as a member of management were typically those of the catering contractors and the suppliers of medical and safety equipment. Subsequently, when the emphasis switched to industrial relations, advice and assistance on industrial negotiations became available from full time specialists provided by the employers' federations and similar organizations. Soon after the second world war the personnel manager became increasingly involved in the planning of managerial resources and, correspondingly, specialist services emerged in areas such as management training and development and the installation of coherent salary structures and associated fringe benefits. Given the heavy emphasis in the 1960s and 1970s, at both national and company level, on the need for more efficient deployment of labour power, it is hardly surprising that specialist services have become established in recruitment, selection and human resource power planning.

The prevailing pattern and scale of external support services reflect the demand for specialist knowledge and concentrated experience which many individual companies can no longer justify as an internal resource. Furthermore, the characteristic attitudes of managers towards external services correlate with the stage of development of that particular branch of management. When a profession or a management function is long established, it becomes normal practice to make judicious use of the services of specialist practitioners when these are appropriate. Company secretaries, for example, would be deemed to have failed if they did not recognize the circumstances in which it was prudent to supplement their own personal skills with outside assistance from solicitors, auditors, taxation experts, legal advisers etc. Similar considerations apply to the chief engineer, the sales manager, the research manager, the medical officer—in fact to every occupational sphere around which exists a systematized body of professional knowledge. General practitioners cannot have, and are not expected to have, the same facilities as specialist consultants. They can be expected to be familiar with the specialist services which are available, to know how and when to use them and to exercise professional judgement about their possible relevance and comparative merits. So it is in the personnel field. Specialist services can supplement the skills of the personnel manager but they do not supplant them. In appropriate circumstances, they can aid job performance but they cannot do the job for her. As personnel management itself evolves into a fully-fledged profession, the range of specialist support services will grow and still greater demands will be made on them. However, those of direct relevance to recruitment and selection at the present time can be regarded as falling into broad categories:

    (a) employment agencies
    (b) candidate registers
    (c) advertising agencies
    (d) selection consultants
    (e) outplacement consultants
    (f) executive search consultants
    (g) salary and pensions consultants

In their different ways, each aims to provide a link between prospective employer and prospective candidate.

### (a) Employment agencies

These are not new; what is new is the tremendous number that exist. Virtually all now operate on a commercial basis including the Professional and Executive Recruitment of the Department of Employment. With its computer data bank accessible through terminals throughout the country the PER may give wider coverage than a local agency, or group of agencies, and can be especially useful in identifying pockets of labour in other areas. The PER gives an increasingly professional service from this register, with its qualified and trained consultant staff. It is not cheap but it represents good value for money. Certain professional and quasi-professional bodies also offer to put prospective employers in touch with members who are looking for work; similar services are operated too by some charitable organizations. They do not usually charge a fee or at most a moderate one. These organizations are essentially offering a service to their members and given sufficient information they will try to be selective.

The commercial employment agencies rely on charging the employer an appointment fee, usually about one month's salary, for introducing a candidate who is subsequently engaged. Many offer also to supply temporary staff on a short term basis in which case an hourly or daily rate is charged. Employment agencies tend to specialize in a particular type of employee, such as computer operators, secretaries, nurses etc. They flourish when demand exceeds supply. It is obligatory for all employment agents to register and to be licenced to operate by the Department of Employment. The object of this is to raise operating standards and cut exorbitant fees. It also paves the way for their closure or absorption by the PER which has been demanded by a previous Labour administration.

When notifying a vacancy to an agency it is important to give full information about the nature of the job, the conditions of employment and the qualifications demanded in the candidates. Employment agents cannot reasonably be blamed for submitting unsuitable candidates, if they have been given only the scantiest information to act on. There is a clear onus on the prospective employer to define assessment criteria with a fair degree of precision and, having done so, time wasting can be avoided by impressing on the agency that only candidates with some prior evidence that they meet those criteria will be interviewed. However, standards among agencies still vary very widely and it is up to employers to demand a high standard of performance. Also, no agency will be motivated to provide a top quality service if fees have been forced below an economic level or if the client appears to be miserly. Even so, there are several limiting factors such as:

●   the ability of agency staff to interpret accurately both the employer's specification and the attributes of prospective applicants.

- the number and calibre of people who happen to be on that particular agency's books at that particular moment of time.

- the number of people motivated to move from their present jobs, many of whom may be desperate, lacking initiative or simply wanting careers advice on the cheap.

### (b) Candidate registers

The dividing-line between the employment agency and the candidate register is not a simple one to draw and some firms offer both types of service. However, a number of registers emerged in the 1960s and 1970s which aim to concentrate on candidates with technical qualifications or scientific degrees. In the first instance, the attention of candidates is obtained by offering to circulate particulars of their careers to a large number of employers. Each employer pays a subscription in order to receive an issue of the register (or a series of issues) containing brief particulars of the candidates but not giving their names or addresses: employers can then go through the register and ask the publisher to put him in touch with any candidate they wish to interview. Methods vary, but an appointment fee is usually payable if a candidate is engaged.

Generally, the publisher does not pre-select candidates other than by confining eligibility to those who claim to possess the prescribed qualifications and by grouping the entries into a number of sub-categories. The task of assessment is left entirely to the prospective employer. There is a practical problem in getting value from any register, since it may be necessary to read through numerous papers in the hope of discovering one candidate who appears to be suitably qualified for a current job; even then, there is no means of knowing whether the candidate will be interested in that particular position in that company. Inclusion in the register merely indicates that someone is interested in moving from her/his present job. The register technique is more likely to appeal to younger candidates who have recently qualified than to older people with several years' experience; to the professional who brackets himself with others under a generic label such as chemist or metallurgist rather than to the individual who has achieved a position of significance; and to the prospective candidate who aims to explore the job market by casting her bread upon the waters rather than to the more senior executive who is determined to sit tight until her interest is aroused by a specific appointment which calls for particular qualifications. Although the register technique offers protection to the candidate by withholding the name and address, it seems likely that some may be inhibited from using it by a fear that they might be identified from the details of their careers.

*(c)  Advertising agencies*
Few companies spending over £20,000 per annum on recruitment advertising will have any difficulty in finding an advertising agency willing to work with them. More difficulty is likely to be experienced in determining what standard of service it is reasonable to expect. There are few books and hardly any training courses to help the practising personnel manager to get the best results from advertising, and from an advertising agency. It is worth remembering several basic propositions.
(i) Advertising agencies rely for their main source of income on the discounts they receive from the publications in which their clients' advertisements appear. These discounts vary, but are usually between 10 and 15 per cent of the value of the advertising. It is possible therefore, for the personnel manager to estimate how much income the agency derives from his or her company's advertising and to consider whether the quality of the service matches up to that figure.
(ii) The personnel manager has an obligation to ensure that his company's expenditure on recruitment advertising is spent productively. It is a curious paradox that in a firm where he is not permitted to authorize even £1,000 on capital equipment, the personnel manager can often sanction advertising commitments aggregating to tens of thousands of pounds per annum. It is incumbent on him to see that value for money is obtained. The first and obvious step is to maintain systematic records of the cost per appointment and to be on the lookout constantly for signs of rising trends. It is futile to seek economies by sending advertisements directly to the newspapers since the amount charged for the space will be precisely the same. Indeed, additional indirect costs are likely to be incurred, since every agency relieves its clients of the financial burden of handling the administrative aspects of his

advertising. The more hopeful course lies in keeping the agency constantly on its toes.

(iii) At least once a year, the personnel manager should hold a thorough stocktaking review with the agency at which the previous year's advertising activities, and the agency's contribution to them should be scrutinized closely. If the agency should lack the resources to provide the desired standard of service, the personnel manager need have no compunction about considering a change to another agency.

What then should be the keynote of the client-agency relationship? Since the object is efficient recruitment, the agency should be concerned about filling jobs and not merely with filling advertising spaces. It must understand what the personnel manager is aiming to achieve and help her to achieve it. The personnel manager and the advertising agency have complementary roles. The personnel manager looks at the jobs to be filled from a vantage point within the company and the agency looks at them through the eyes of the potential candidate who is outside; and the personnel manager contributes an intimate knowledge of those jobs, whilst the agency contributes its knowledge of the candidate market and how best to communicate with it. Thus a continuous pooling of ideas and knowledge should be taking place. The agency should offer advice on how to advertise and where to advertise, but the final decisions must always remain the prerogative of the personnel manager. If this two-way flow of information is not present, it is unlikely that a company is getting full value for money. The hardest part of the personnel manager's task is to word the advertisements so that they convey all that she wants them to convey to potential candidates who, by definition, lack her framework of knowledge.

How can the quality of an advertising agency service be assessed? The administrative advantages should not be underestimated but these are common to all agencies: only one copy of the text need be supplied no matter how many publications are to be used; the agency will book space; prepare the layout and typography; read and correct proofs; verify that the right advertisement has appeared in the right publications at the right time; and only one cheque has to be raised to settle the agency's monthly account. But this is the minimum service which all agencies can provide. What criteria can be used to differentiate between good and indifferent service? Since the agency's function is to help the personnel manager to communicate with potential candidates about jobs that have to be filled, it is relevant to ask some further questions:

● Is recruitment the agency's main business or a casual side-line?

● How much does the agency representative understand about personnel selection?

● Do they appreciate what kind of people are being sought and what might influence them to change jobs?

● Are they competent to advise on the wording of the advertisements?

● Do they offer advice on which media to use and, if so, on what facts about comparative pulling-power is this advice based?

● Have all advertisements been published accurately and promptly?

● Has the quality of response been good enough?

● Does the agency offer any special service such as panel advertisements or a confidential reply service under their own well-known house style?

A rigorous check-list such as this is needed in order to compare the agency's services from one year to another and also to compare them with the alternative services available. Agencies differ greatly in the calibre of staff they employ and, since everything which an agency does has to be done by people, this is an important yardstick to apply. Historically, most advertising agencies were established to support the marketing functions of management and to assist the sales manager to boost company's sales. They tend to be staffed largely by people whose knowledge and experience is centred in the marketing field. In some cases, their involvement in recruitment is subsidiary and incidental to this. It is a salutary thought that whereas specialist services in product advertising have existed since the 1930s, comparable services in recruitment advertising emerged only in the 1960s. A company's marketing director expects the agency, as a matter of course, to contribute specialist skills and concentrated experience to the solution of the company's unique marketing problems. The agency is not concerned only with getting the advertisements printed: it is expected to know about the probable demand for a product, to understand and to analyse consumer preferences and to prepare draft advertisements in the light of its client's overall marketing strategy. Should the personnel manager be satisfied with less? The financial relationship is the same. Since the adoption of display techniques for recruitment advertising, there are many companies whose annual expenditure on recruitment advertising now exceeds their expenditure on product advertising. But the standard of agency service will not necessarily have improved. Personnel managers have received, and will continue to receive, only as good a service as they themselves have demanded. Unless they are exacting in their demands and insist that their advertising agency acquires an informed insight into their recruitment problems and contributes impartially to their solution, they will be handicapped in the task of recruiting effectively.

## (d) Selection consultants

Consultants cannot survive in business if they merely duplicate the personnel manager's role. The consultant's true value lies in supplementing the skills available within their client's organization.

Consultancy firms specializing in the recruitment and selection field did not exist before 1955. Since then, hundreds have been set up. Some have flourished but many have faded from the scene. The successful ones tend to be 'problem-solving' organizations and their strength lies in the concentrated experience which they can relate to their clients' needs. They are essentially client-oriented in outlook. The pattern of services has widened progressively. Industry is still discovering, sometimes by cautious experiment, that external advice and assistance can be obtained to meet a wide range of recruitment and selection situations. During these years, new generic terms such as 'management selection' and 'selection consultants' have been added to the management vocabulary. Simultaneously, consultancy services in allied fields, such as training, salaries administration, security etc, have also been developing rapidly, but lie outside the scope of this book.

The principal activity of selection consultants, usually a division of a general management consultancy in the 1950s, was to help companies to fill senior executive appointments, and this continues to be one of their major functions. At first, it gave rise to some misgivings, based usually on the mistaken assumption that the vital task of picking a firm's key executives was being handed over to outsiders. In fact, the more reputable consultants have always emphasized that the client must make the ultimate decision on which person to appoint, whilst relieving them of much of the work culminating in that decision. No-one can make a satisfactory choice unless there are satisfactory candidates to choose from; the consultant's contribution usually owes as much to the facility for assembling a strong field of candidates as it does to an assessment skill in differentiating between those candidates.

*(e)  Outplacement consultants*
This decade has seen the rise of 'executive career counsellors', part of whose service is to help candidates market themselves. They will send copies of curricula vitae to prospective employers who may find them of interest. This is a free service to the employer: the candidates pay the counsellor.

*(f)  Executive search*
The 1960s saw the advent and growth of many specialist selection consultants. Some of these were general and some specialized in certain functions or certain levels of appointment. Others began to broaden their base and introduced special services for younger executives; some set up their own specialist advertising agencies. Several made a real attempt to offer a continuing service to their clients as opposed to *ad hoc* assistance with a specific appointment. A new form of service has emerged strongly in the 1970s: the executive search consultant. With its roots in the United States this type of service was slow to catch on in the United Kingdom and the rest of Europe. Partly assisted by over-full employment and partly, curiously, by unemployment, this type of service has expanded

enormously in the 1970s. Briefly, the executive search consultant (or 'headhunter') approaches the candidates directly. They do this by a form of market research to identify possible candidates; by agreement they will then either canvass all possible candidates or confine their activities to the best people between, say, certain age limits. At first this type of service was challenged as being unethical. However, this was investigated by the Edinburgh Group of the Institute of Personnel Management who reported in the November 1969 issue of the IPM Journal that this type of service was no more unethical than a recruitment advertisement. However, practices do vary. In the 1980s the executive search approach has become well-established and much recruitment activity is termed 'search' precisely for its up-market appeal. True executive search is a time-consuming and therefore expensive business; it is not simply a matter of tapping a secret data bank of top talent. Neither does it rely on a register of people who have contacted them over the years (though every executive search concern keeps records of people who they have assessed in the past or who have been strongly recommended to them in a special context). The executive search firm sets out to identify afresh for each assignment who best meets an exacting specification by searching out those with a high reputation in very specific areas. Consultants must have the skill to identify these people; to obtain confidential verification, or the reverse, of their tentative conclusions, and to approach senior people on level terms in an atmosphere of considerable trust. They have to guide their clients who are not used to recruiting at this level and be able to negotiate the remuneration package—say for a company chairman with an international reputation. True search only works satisfactorily at senior levels where the number of possible candidates is small—a maximum of 200 say. This is the reason why search is confined to very senior levels, such as board or head of function appointments. Below this level it can be a time-consuming, hit and miss affair—unless one is dealing in a closely defined industry where reputations are easily made and widely known, eg publishing, advertising, or sport.

### (g) *Salary and pensions consultants*
Although largely outside the scope of this book, reference should be made to the growing number of consultants who offer specialist

services in these areas as they are of increasing relevance to those involved in recruitment. Most salary surveys give only very broad guidance when it comes to attracting a specific group of people to specific jobs in specific companies. Moreover, both salary and pension provisions are becoming more variable and genuinely negotiable. Share options may also be available at senior levels. Expert technical advice may need to be sought from outside from time to time. At the time of writing, it is unusual to obtain all of this from one firm, and that usually only on a continuous basis, but it is likely that this will soon become a service available on an occasional basis as all the others.

The types of service available may conveniently be divided between those of a continuing and those of an *ad hoc* nature.

*Services of a continuing nature*

These are characterized by a close personal relationship sustained between an individual consultant and an individual firm; and the consultant can, in a sense, be regarded as a part time member of its staff. He or she is available to give advice at short notice and is able to do so because she or he has an up to date grasp of the company's background gained from frequent visits and meetings. In some cases they may fulfil the function of personnel director and their advice may be sought on all aspects of personnel policy. Generally, his or her brief will be more narrowly defined. It may, for example, be concerned with human resource planning or with management succession and development, in which case a second opinion may be given on all short-listed candidates for key posts, whether from outside or inside the company. In other cases they may be retained to advise on psychological testing or to train members of the company's staff in recruitment and selection methods. Thus professional personnel skills are brought within the reach of the smaller and medium sized firms which cannot afford or could not attract a senior personnel manager as a full time employee. By retaining a consultant for perhaps one or two days a month, they are able in effect to share with a number of other firms the cost of having access to widely-based experience. When entering into arrangements of this kind, it is important to ensure that the consultant's precise terms of reference are agreed in advance and that a written quotation is obtained specifying the amount of the retainer fee and exactly what it covers.

Particularly relevant are the advertising agency services available through some selection consultants. Since these are financed mainly by discounts received from publications, consultancy fees are not usually charged to regular clients. By channelling its recruitment advertising through one of these specialist agencies, a company can obtain all the normal facilities expected from a conventional advertising agency plus, in effect, the part time services of a recruitment consultant. At no extra cost, the consultant's knowledge of the current recruitment market is built into all the company's recruitment activities on a continuing basis. Supplementary services covering the design and preparation of employment handbooks and careers literature may also be provided, and a separate fee is usually quoted for these.

### *Services of an* ad hoc *nature*

It is virtually impossible to have constantly available within one company sufficient full time staff with the precise blend of knowledge needed to cater for each and every recruitment contingency that might arise. To do so would be impractical and grossly uneconomic. On the other hand, every company must be reasonably self sufficient and must aim to rely on its own resources to deal with the mainstream of its recruitment activities. By programming ahead, it is quite feasible to have most of the appropriate skills available within the personnel department at most times. Even so, situations will occasionally arise in which it is desirable to augment these skills. Sometimes this may be because the sheer volume of recruitment work at peak periods is beyond the physical capacity of the full time staff, and additional capacity may be needed for only a few weeks. On other occasions, special techniques or facilities may be needed to resolve an unusual recruitment problem. Consultancy services designed to help with these different types of contingencies can be obtained.

Reputable consultants will always endeavour to give honest advice on whether and, if so, how they can help in any given situation. A fee is not usually payable for an exploratory discussion nor need this imply any obligation. Even so, from the outset, the prospective client ought to have a reasonably clear idea of why consultancy assistance might be of value. There is no sense in paying a consultant to do what could equally well be done by the company's own staff. The consultant's role is to supplement a company's own resources, not to supplant them. The proposed form and scale of any consultancy assignment should always be evaluated in the light of the actual contribution which the company genuinely needs from that consultant.

The immediate problem may be to do with internal promotion. Consultants can provide an additional and impartial assessment of the comparative strengths and weaknesses of several employees who are either being considered for promotion to a specific vacancy or whose general potential for future development is to be assessed. They can also advise on how those present employees compare with candidates who might be found elsewhere. This external yardstick of comparison can be especially useful when the company's own assessment standards are based on only a small sample of people in that category. Naturally, the consultants must first obtain a clear cut understanding of the particular job requirements. Having done so, they will be in a position to recommend whether or not psychological tests would strengthen the assessment procedures; and they will be qualified usually to administer and interpret such tests, if appropriate.

*How selection consultants work*

Perhaps the most remarkable feature of the past decades has been the establishment of the consultant as a confidential third party between prospective employer and prospective candidate. This intermediary role is one of considerable delicacy. It presupposes a high degree of mutual trust; but its practical value also depends on the consultant's skill in making well-informed judgements about the job to be filled and about the availability and attitudes of suitably experienced people. He or she provides a confidential assessment and communication link between the job and the potential candidate market and has to understand both.

The first practical step, therefore, is for the consultant to visit the company for a confidential discussion about the recruitment problem to familiarize him/herself with what the company does and with the background to the proposed appointment. Until this process of fact-finding, analysis and diagnosis has been carried out constructive guidance cannot be offered about the most effective means of finding someone suitably equipped to do that particular job in that particular company. The consultant's impartial drawing up of the job/person specifications, coupled with advice about the candidate market and prevailing salary levels, may sometimes point to a necessary change of emphasis in the composition of the job itself. The consultant's report usually includes a summary of the exact job to be filled, as well as recommendations on the most economical and effective way of filling it. It will include a precise specification of the type of person to be sought, recommendations on the terms to be offered and detailed proposals on how and where to advertise. The client must decide whether to accept those recommendations; and whether to authorize the consultant to go ahead with the assignment. Generally, there is no binding obligation on either client or on the consultant to proceed beyond this initial stage.

If the job is to be advertised, it may be published in the consultant's name, in which case the client's identity may either be included in the advertisement or withheld from it. No consultant can attach a name to an advertisement without incurring obligations to both client and candidates. Those obligations—whether explicit or implicit—must be honoured by the client as well as by the consultant, whose reputation is a vital factor in his or her success. The consultant's direct involvement in the later selection stages will vary, depending on how much the client is able and willing to undertake; and this, in turn, may depend on the level and type of job. The wording of the advertisement will reflect the form of service being provided. In certain situations, the consultant's role is primarily that of attracting initial applications from suitable candidates; in other situations, they may also be involved in carrying out most of the assessment work, since this may be inseparable from the further contributions which the client needs from them.

*Junior and middle management*
For jobs in the junior and middle management range, an abbreviated form of intermediary service will often suffice. Procedures vary. The most elementary version is where the candidate applies *through* the consultant, who guarantees to withhold that application from any companies nominated in a stop-list enclosed by the candidate. Protection is offered against the risk

of applying inadvertently to a past or present employer; but the stimulus to apply depends otherwise on the information contained in the advertisement. A significant refinement is for the consultant's advertisement to indicate that additional information about that appointment will be sent on request. This offers the positive advantage to the potential candidate that she or he has merely to give his or her name and address; it can be subsequently decided whether it is worth submitting a formal applicatio.. o. not after the more detailed supplementary information has been read. Fees charged for these services (and variants of them) are often no more than might otherwise be spent on a box number advertisement. A precise fee quotation should always be obtained before an assignment is authorized.

*Top management appointments*
More senior appointments sometimes call for more sophisticated methods. Senior executives have to be wooed assiduously. They already occupy positions of considerable responsibility and may not be consciously looking for another job. Even if they are, they cannot afford the risk of it becoming known. They may be disinclined to apply directly to another company, unless they are reasonably sure that they want that particular job. Here the selection or executive search consultant has a choice: the job may be advertised over the consultant's name or candidates may be approached by search, or a combination of the two may be used. Whichever method is adopted the preliminary stages are the same. If the appointment is advertised the same procedures will be adopted as for middle management appointments. The executive search consultant will begin by identifying the likely sources of potential candidates. This will be carried out through the consultant's own records, through official directories, through contacts and through a study of relevant professional trade journals. Executive search is only economic when the possible number of candidates is, say, below 200 and where they are readily identifiable as individuals. For this reason executive search is not normally conducted below a salary level of £25,000, although in special instances it can certainly be done at lower levels; advertising will be generally far more efficient at levels in excess of £10,000 a year. Again, search is not so effective for the under 30s as it is for older

people. The search consultant has then to determine which of the candidates stand out above the rest and will seek to probe their professional reputation before approaching, say, a short list of about 10 people. Finally, the consultant will present the client with a short list of three or four people. Whichever course is adopted, the consultant has to sell the job proposition to the candidate and a fair amount of negotiation ensues.

Many candidates are attracted by this form of recruitment. They like the informality, the position of equality between consultant and candidate and the opportunity to discuss with an impartial but informed third party the pros and cons of taking this step. A candidate can withdraw without embarrassment if he or she decides that the job is not suitable, alternatively, if his or her name is included in the final short list, it is with prior agreement and it can be assumed that he or she has but a one in four chance of being offered that appointment. Of course, the highest level of confidentiality prevails throughout the entire exercise. The consultant saves the client considerable time, undertaking the time-consuming work of reading applications or evaluating career histories and conducting the bulk of the interviews. The consultant also provides a specialist skill in attracting candidates and assessing them, plus the reassurance of an informed, objective second opinion. Fees for this type of service vary. Where advertising is involved, they will be between 15 and $22\frac{1}{2}$ per cent of the appointed candidate's first year salary. Executive search is more expensive and can be obtained rarely for less than 25 per cent, more usually in excess of 30 per cent, of the appointed candidate's first year's salary. Often no results are guaranteed and the full fee is payable when the search has been completed, say after a notional three months. If the search has to be conducted internationally, the fee may be as high as 50 per cent of the first year's salary, plus the consultant's expenses.

*A guide to consultancy services*
The British Institute of Management used to maintain a register of management consultants, including particulars of those firms which offer consultancy services in the recruitment and selection field. A management buy-out has ensured its continuity under the

name of its former operator, Anne Mallach.[1] Consultants offering a range of management services enable this service to follow up major assignments so as to evaluate their effectiveness in the eyes of their clients. Generally it is a case of 'horses for courses' and suitable recommendations will be made. Other useful sources are professional bodies, and the publication, *The Executive Grapevine* (see *Bibliography*, page 160).

[1]Anne Mallach, Management Consultancy Information Service, 38 Blenheim Avenue, Gants Hill, Ilford, Essex IG2 6JQ. Tel. 01 554 4695.

# Reflections on recruitment

These *Reflections* focus attention on five different recruitment situations and illustrate some characteristic pitfalls. They emphasize the importance of looking at recruitment 'through the eyes of the candidate' and of anticipating the attitudes and reactions of prospective employees. Each *Reflection* depicts a separate situation, hence there is no need to read them in sequence. The various episodes, when considered as a whole, also show how general principles about recruitment in practice must be applied sensitively and sensibly to meet widely differing circumstances.

    I    The school leaver
   II    The factory operative
  III    The office worker
   IV    The graduate
    V    The manager

*Author's Note* The characters in these *Reflections* are wholly fictitious, they are unrelated to any people or companies with similar names. Alas, the events portrayed happen every day.

## The school leaver

Local school leavers should be a firm's best source of supply of potential technicians, sales representatives and operatives. To school leavers the act of starting work is a leap into the unknown. Their knowledge of the work available locally is derived largely from hearsay and much of that will seem dull and uninspiring. With improvements in the educational system, the school leavers are becoming more discriminating when seeking their first job. Some employers fail to realize this as John Ashton was to discover:

"I'm John Ashton and I live in a council house in Wythenshawe. My dad's a fitter in an engineering firm at Trafford Park. My mum works part time in a school canteen. Ian, my brother, is an apprentice draughtsman and our Sally works in a shop. Sally and Bob, her husband, are living with us until she has a baby so they can get higher up the list for a council house.

"I go to a comprehensive and will be sitting for GCE in maths and English this summer. I'm also taking CSE in maths, English, general science, technical drawing, metalwork and geography—in case I don't get GCE! I've been a prefect since September and play in the school football team—usually as inside right. I'm not so badly off for cash now, as I put some time in as a pump attendant at a nearby garage at weekends. At Christmas I got my first motor bike (second hand) and Joe up at the garage has helped me improve it a bit.

"When I leave school in July, I want to be a fitter like my dad. Everyone tells me to get a trade behind me, as a sort of insurance, but I want to do better than that eventually. I don't know what exactly, but better—a white collar job, perhaps. The careers teacher had us all in last week to find out what we want to do when we leave school. I told him and he said, 'Get a good training. Join a firm with a good training scheme, like Supreme Engineering Company; you know, the one that showed us round their works just after Christmas. I wouldn't advise the Bricklands Machine Company, though. They won't let us take any of our pupils round and I reckon they must be ashamed of the place. Keep away from Dodgson's too. They call it an apprenticeship there, but they've no proper training school and there are no indentures. Go and see Mrs Shingle, the youth employment officer, and pay attention to what she says.' Mrs Shingle gave me some green cards to take to several firms. This is what happened.

"The Clarefield Precision works isn't far off, so I went there first. At the main gate I was told to go to 'the Employment' and I showed my green card to a woman inside. She gave me a form and told me to fill it in. She also gave me a booklet to look at. I managed to fill in the form—it didn't want much and most of it like 'previous jobs' didn't apply to me as I haven't done any. I waited about half an hour, then her 'phone buzzed and she took me in to see Mr Johnson, I think his name was.

"He had quite a nice office, though the chairs were a bit

scruffy. He told me to sit down and started to read my form. After a few minutes (it seemed like hours) he said:

— So your name's John Ashton.

— Yes.

— And you live at—I can't read this—No 2 Hill Rise, Wythenshawe. Is that right?

— Yes.

— And you go to Wythenshawe High School.

— Yes.

— And you're taking GCE maths and English this summer; and CSE maths, English, general science, technical drawing, metalwork and geography as well?

— Yes.

— Hmm. I see and how do you think you got on in your CSE?

— I think I'll pass.

— All of them?

— Yes.

— I see. And what about your GCE?

— I don't know.

— I see you list motor bike repairs as your main hobby.

— Well, I've got a bike—bought it at Christmas and Joe at the garage where I work on Saturdays . . .

— You work on Saturdays?

— Yes.

— Why didn't you say so before?

— I didn't think . . .

— Well you should. If you're going to be an apprentice, you've got to learn to think.

— Yes.

— Well, get on with it.

— Get on with what?

— Your bike, lad.

— Oh, Joe helped me improve it up a bit.

— Um—and now you tear up the estate at weekends, I suppose. *(No answer)*

— Why do you want to become an apprentice?

— Because my dad's a fitter and Tom, my brother, is a draughtsman and says it's all right and I want a trade behind me.

— Trade behind you?

woman there really tried to help me sort something out and I felt I could talk freely to her. She didn't treat me like a child either. Mind you, she hasn't sent me anything yet.

During the next week things began to look up. Christine received three invitations to interview: one from a bank, another from the local Inland Revenue offices and another from an accounts department of a large department store. It would mean taking more time off, but luckily one was on her half-day. In due course she attended all three interviews and reported back to George:
— I went to the bank first. It was very awe-inspiring until I went round the back and saw the girls at work. The manager was very nice and kind, and said that they could consider me for some computer work. I would need training, of course.
— Sounds very good to me. Did you take it?
— No—because she said she'd write and let me know. If she'd offered me a job on the spot I'd probably have taken it, but now I've seen the others I don't think I will. The hours would be just as bad as they are now. The work was all right and she made no bones about my engagement since I could always come back again after I'd, well, had a family. I can't really say why I don't like it, looking back. They seemed rather a stuck-up crowd and I don't think I would fit in very well. I suppose that's the only real reason.
— After that I went to the Inland Revenue. What a contrast! Masses of people all crammed into scruffy offices sorting out income tax claims. The inspector was nice enough and said they're moving to new offices, but I really couldn't see myself working there, George.
— The hours are quite good though aren't they, and you get good holidays—and it's very secure.
— Yes, that's true, but I simply couldn't stand being cooped up in there all day.
— The other one—the department store—was quite different. I saw the staff officer first. She was quite young and discussed the whole thing with me thoroughly. Then she took me to the accounts department. The offices were new and clean and the people seemed quite nice. All the machines were new and everyone was busy. The hours wouldn't be much better but the pay is good and after a while you can get a discount on

— Yes—to fall back on.
— So you don't want to stay on the bench?
— No.
— Well, John, there's no point in going any further. We want lads who're prepared to work and work hard here. You take my advice and don't try to run before you can walk. Get a trade if you can, but don't go bothering about promotion at your age: if you're any good the firm'll look after you. Good morning.
— Good morning. Oh, do you want the green card?
— Aye, I'll send it back to the youth employment officer.
— I see. I'll be off then. Good morning.

"My second card was for the Electrical and Mechanical Engineering Company. That didn't last long either. I had to go to the personnel department—all nicely set out like a doctor's surgery with books and flowers and things. I was told to make myself at home, after giving my name to the chap in uniform.

"When it was my turn, I went in. It was a nice comfortable-looking office and the woman—Mrs Whatever-it-was (I didn't catch her name)—seemed friendly. She shook hands and told me to sit down.

— Well, what can I do for you?
— I want an apprenticeship.
— What sort of apprenticeship?
— In engineering.
— Any particular trade?
— A fitter or something like that.
— Do you know anything about fitting, what it involves, the different types and so on?
— My dad's a fitter—so I think I do.
— Good. How well are you doing at school?
— Well, I'm taking GCE in maths and English, and CSE in maths, English, technical drawing, metalwork, general science and geography this summer. I hope to get the CSEs, but don't know about the GCEs.
— Fine. Well now, I'm going to give you a form to fill in and a booklet telling you all about us and our training scheme. Then I want you to come back on Tuesday next week and sit some tests. Have you any questions you'd like to ask me?

— How much do I get?

— I can't remember exactly, but it's all in the booklet.

— Do I have to take these tests?

— Yes.

— I haven't any more questions.

— All right then. Let the commissionaire have your form when you've filled it in and we'll see you on Tuesday at 8.30 am. OK?

— Yes.

— So long, then.

— So long.

"I went outside to the waiting room and had a quick look at the form—there were eight pages of it asking questions about my dad, my mum, whether they were married, divorced and so on. A bit of cheek, I thought—and it would take me hours to complete it. I told the bloke I'd take it home and bring it in tomorrow.

"I looked at my other green cards. I decided to go next to the Supreme Engineering Company. I went to the main gate and one of the chaps showed me where the personnel department was. They took my green card and told me to sit down and wait a minute. It was a nice room, clean and tidy with pictures on the walls. Photographs of some of the things they make there—looked quite good too. The secretary said:

— Mr Smith will see you now. Would you like to leave your coat here?

"I went in. Mr Smith was the chap who showed us round before—leastways he was in charge—apprentices actually took us round, and he'd given us a talk: quite interesting it was. He got up, shook hands and asked me what I wanted to do after I'd left school. He talked in a friendly way about the training scheme, what I would do and so on. Then he said:

— I'd like you to let us have some information about yourself on this form and then come back for another interview next week. What we do is give you some tests and then a couple of us will have a chat with you. We do this for all people like yourself. The tests tell us if you have any special abilities that you haven't had a chance to develop at school. This helps us to see whether you would make a good fitter—or a better machinist—or perhaps might become a draughtsman or something like that. They're specially designed for people like yourself, and I don't think you'll find them too bad at all. And then we have another talk with you to find out just what you really want to do and give you a chance to ask us any questions you like. Now is there anything you would like to ask me at this stage?

— Well, no, I think you've told me all I want to know at the moment. Thank you very much.

"When I was outside I glanced at the form he'd given me. It didn't look too bad—but there would be tests again. Still, they didn't sound too bad from the way he'd explained them. Perhaps I've got some hidden talent! Not likely—but it's worth a try. I'll fill this one in tonight and see what happens before I go trailing around any more places. But I suppose I'd better see what dad's got to say first."

*Commentary*

School leavers, especially those of above average ability, are perceptive and sensitive when they visit a succession of different firms. John's reactions illustrate some practical points which are often overlooked. His reception and the attitudes of the people he meets tell him a lot about the firm. They reveal something of the social framework within which he might shortly be asked to work. His first impressions stick fast and colour everything else. John will respond to a reasonable challenge inside a known framework, but will fight shy of the unknown. His reaction to tests is fairly common. The subject always needs to be introduced carefully even at a preliminary meeting, as well as when the tests are later being administered. It is important to recognize that the interviewer needs a deep understanding of the adolescent's world. Initial communication and rapport are difficult to establish. The interviewer belongs to the 'they' group, the authoritarian adult world mistrusted by so many young people. Understanding and insight will help the interviewer to make a realistic appraisal of John through sensitive questioning and probing of attitudes. It is necessary to guard against the danger of interpreting too superficially the dogmatic utterances which many youngsters are prone to blurt out.

The successful recruitment of school leavers requires a long term plan. The well-informed personnel officer will realize that most school leavers take their parents' advice, with careers teachers and youth employment officers supplying information and acting as liaison officers. (Proper vocational guidance is virtually impossible when the youth employment officer can allow only ten minutes per applicant.) Time invested by a firm in ensuring that it merits a good local reputation as an employer repays ample dividends. This can be assisted by regular contacts with careers teachers and youth employment officers; taking part in local careers conventions; talks to schools; inviting school parties to tour the factory; and by making information available through the local newspapers. Even more important, the youngsters already employed will influence the attitudes of others in the district. It is easy enough to agree with these abstract propositions, but if John Ashton applied to your firm today, what would be his reactions?

  (i) Would he already have heard favourable comments from relations, friends, careers teacher and youth employment officer?
 (ii) Would he receive an encouraging reception?
(iii) Would you have a suitable application form?
 (iv) Would your recruitment literature mean anything to him?
  (v) Would he be seen by a trained interviewer chosen for his or her understanding of school leavers and skill in assessment?
 (vi) Would he go away feeling that he was wanted and would be fairly assessed?

## The factory operative

The major part of the recruitment activity in many companies consists of finding and engaging factory operatives and other shop floor employees. During periods of expansion or high labour turnover, this work is going on all the time. In spite of this, or perhaps because of it, recruitment arrangements sometimes allow the most alarming things to happen. This is so particularly if inadequately trained staff are exposed to severe pressure of work. A casual or disorganized approach proves very costly in the long run. On reading the exploits of Millie Scattergood, most personnel

officers will indignantly protest "It couldn't happen here." They
may well be right; but some weaknesses creep into even the most
efficient employment departments from time to time.

Ms Pritchard was very busy. It was Monday morning and she
had a waiting room full of applicants. For payroll vacancies she did
not use application forms, nor had she anyone to look up in her
records of previous employees. Otherwise, she would have seen one
card dated 3 9 '78 and signed J G Chance. It read "Millie
Scattergood should not be re-employed without reference to me".
Mr Chance was a foreman then, now he was works manager.
Millie's reappearance had been prompted by an advertisement in
the local paper.

---

# WHY NOT COME OUT TO WORK AGAIN?

In 5 weeks you could earn enough to buy a new
cooker. In 10 weeks enough to buy a twin-tub
washer. In 20 weeks enough for a holiday in the
Bahamas!
Come and see us and learn something to your
advantage.

Call and see Ms G Pritchard,
Personnel Officer

**WRAP-IT-UP QUICKLY COMPANY**
Rugby

---

Ms Pritchard sighed and pressed her buzzer. Millie walked in.
She sat down as close to Ms Pritchard as possible, so that she could
see anything that was written down.

— Good morning Miss . . . er . . . Mrs . . . ?
— Mrs Scattergood.
— Mrs Scattergood?
— Yes. I've come for a job. Harry Jackson said he'd give me one
   in his department.

— Well, Mrs Scattergood, I don't think we've any vacancies in that department. But we do . . .
— Oh, yes you have. Harry told me that one of his girls is being moved to another machine and I could have her job. I saw him on Saturday night in the King's Arms.
— Did he? It's the first I've heard of it, but I'll have a word with him in a few minutes. Now, what experience . . .

The telephone rang and she broke off to answer it.

— Yes, Harry. She's with me now.

Ms Pritchard tried desperately to wave Millie outside, but Millie pretended not to understand and remained glued to her seat.

— Well, Harry, you might have told me before. She tells me you promised her a job on Saturday. I think you'd better see her and explain the position. I'll send her up now. Experience? Oh yes I think so. (Millie nodded as if to say 'I know all there is to know about injection moulding').

A confused Ms Pritchard replaced the telephone.

— Well, Mrs Scattergood, if you'll wait outside a moment I'll arrange for someone to take you up to the department.
— What's it worth?
— I beg your pardon?
— What's the rate for the job?
— How do I know. I don't even know what the *job* is. You'd better ask Mr Jackson.

Ten minutes later the office junior took Millie up to the department. The interview with Harry was brief; brief and painful for Harry; brief and rewarding for Millie.

— Hallo, Harry.
— Hallo, Millie. Hang on a minute while I just finish this.
— All right. Oh, there's our Rosie. Is it all right if I say hallo to her while I'm waiting?
— Yes, I suppose so.

Millie tripped across to Rosie.

— Here, Rosie, what's the job like that young Sheila Smith's doing? Harry says she'll be moving and I can have it.
— She seems to sit there and just twiddle a few knobs. There doesn't seem much to it, as far as I can see.
— Is it hot?
— No, not really. No hotter than the oven!
— Sitting down, isn't it?
— Yes, all the time.
— Near you?
— Yes. Leastways if I shift myself along the bench a bit . . . What's the rate?
— I don't know yet—I'll have to ask Harry.
— Didn't Pritchard tell you?
— She didn't know anything about it.
— That's even better: tell Harry it's £2.30; so far, Harry's only had a girl on it at £2.10. Tell him that's what you thought Pritchard said. If he swallows it, we'll have some fun.
— Right. I'd better go. Harry's waiting for me.


— Sorry Harry. Well, now about this job. Reckon I could do it with my hands tied behind my back.
— Ever done it before?
— Well, not exactly. But from what I can see, it's no more difficult than cooking Bert's lunch. I've done similar jobs, you know.
— Oh. The trouble is, Millie, that I haven't definitely arranged to move young Sheila yet: it's going to be difficult.
— Yes, but you can manage that Harry, if I know you. My husband, Bert, says it's good for the youngsters to move around a bit.
— Yes, I dare say he does. Well, I'll have a word with Mr Chance.
— Mr Chance? Can't you run your own department without him putting his big nose in?
— Yes, of course . . . All right, Millie. I'll see what I can do.
— Does that mean I can start?
— Just give me half an hour to think about it. You go back to personnel and I'll give them a ring.

— Sounds like you're trying to get out of it to me.

— No, that's not it.

— Then why not say so now?

— Look here, Millie . . . Oh all right, you can have the job. I'll tell personnel.

— I understand the rate's £2.30.

— Who told you that? Sounds a bit high to me.

— That's what Ms Pritchard said.

— Oh well, she should know. We'll pay you £2.30 plus piece work with 100 per cent guaranteed during the first fortnight's learning time.

— That's great, Harry. I'll just go down to personnel and sign myself in. 'Bye for now.

*Commentary*

There are probably very few personnel departments as badly organized as this one. On the other hand, there are quite a number where this sort of thing is liable to happen during temporary absences or when the personnel officer is very busy. Millie, of course, was pretty shrewd and knew how to turn things to her advantage. But she is not unique: most firms encounter their Millies from time to time. Why did she get away with it? Let us consider a few of the major errors.

The advertisement was woolly. It said nothing about the jobs available not about the terms of employment. Perhaps these had not been really thought out: later events certainly suggest this. Before any advertisement is published, the personnel officer should have a clear idea—preferably in writing—of the jobs to be filled and the sort of people needed, together with rates of pay and other employment conditions. If Ms Pritchard had done her homework Millie might never have applied but, even if she had, the interview would have been easier to control. Millie had the advantage throughout and the interview was a farce. She was a difficult person to deal with but Ms Pritchard was courting disaster. Contrary to her belief, application forms for factory employees are not a waste of time. An application form could have told her a great deal about Millie. And if the personnel department had been better organized,

Millie's record of previous employment with the firm would have come to light, and Mr Chance would have been consulted in time. The interview room was badly arranged with Millie sitting so close to Ms Pritchard that she could read notes and overhear her telephone conversation. The latter was disastrous in more ways than one. Any interruption destroys an important feature of an interview—rapport between the parties—and disturbs the flow of information. In this particular case, Ms Pritchard could have firmly insisted that Millie left the room; alternatively, she could have taken the call in the next office if her secretary had been filtering incoming telephone calls.

It is probably tactful to draw a veil over the 'interviews' as such. They neither sought, obtained, nor gave information according to any systematic plan. Ms Pritchard failed to make an effective assessment of Millie, which it was her responsibility to do whether Harry was offering her a job or not. Harry's interview performance was no better. It would be unfair to blame him for being unaware of Mr Chance's note, as Ms Pritchard let him down badly in that respect. To be charitable, we can assume that Harry's firm had overlooked that he was untrained in recruitment. Even some elementary training in employment interviewing would have directed his attention to Millie's lack of experience and to the reasons why she had left her previous jobs. He would have found compelling grounds for withdrawing his rash statement of the previous Saturday—even though Millie was well-known to him socially. Instead he allowed his embarrassment to override his common sense. The wage situation as it developed became an intriguing one! It is always prudent to look up wage rates carefully, as Harry and Miss Pritchard will undoubtedly discover to their cost.

If Millie turns up at your firm when you are taking your well-earned holiday, what exactly will happen? Will there be:

   (i) woolly advertisements which invite her presence?
  (ii) an inadequately staffed personnel department and a distraught, disorganized recruitment officer?
 (iii) an interview situation which she can exploit to her advantage?
  (iv) no provision for application forms to be completed?
   (v) a foreman as inept and untrained as Harry?

## The office worker

Office and clerical vacancies seem difficult to fill. At one time the prospects of security and social status coupled with 'nine to five' hours were sufficient to attract high calibre people to clerical work. Many a managing director of today started his working life 'in the office'. Increased educational opportunities now enable more to go to universities or technical colleges instead. Simultaneously, mechanization and computerization of many office procedures has been changing the nature of the work itself rapidly and radically. Industry and commerce need to employ staff in the office, but their slowness in adapting to these technological and social phenomena might leave people like Christine Owen uncertain of where their future lies.

Christine Owen was born and brought up in a large provincial city in the South of England where her parents owned a small grocery shop. At a private school she had found lessons difficult and was placed consistently well down the class lists. She passed three out of five O levels, history (her favourite subject), geography and biology, and failed mathematics and English. She had been good at arithmetic but weak at algebra and geometry—and her English grammar had never been strong. She left at 16 and got a job in a local travel agency where she did clerical work which included some holiday planning and a fair amount of arithmetic.

Christine is now 19. Money has assumed a new importance in her life and she has resolved to get a better job with shorter hours if possible. Recently she has been going to night school and has passed O level English and mathematics. She also started a course in shorthand and typing but left half way through as her shorthand was hopeless, although her typing was good.

One evening she talked things over with her boyfriend. Secretarial work was out; she was not keen to become a typist; and she did not really like routine clerical work. She wanted something to do with figures and to realize her full market value; she was prepared to undertake a short course of training. Being 'engaged', she felt that no employer would be interested in her even though she did not plan to marry for at least 18 months, and even then would want to work for a year or two before starting a family. George thought that she should at least try to get what she wanted and suggested some sort of office accounting work.

The following evening they worked out a plan of campaign. They would study all the advertisements in the evening and weekend papers; Christine would tour the employment agencies and make enquiries among her friends. They decided against the Department of Employment. "I'm not as desperate as all that", she said.

To start with, things went quite well. Christine replied to some advertisements that appealed to her. Several friends promised to put in a word for her with their bosses and Christine toured the agencies. Attending interviews was not quite so easy. She had only a half-day off per week and soon used up the other 'lieu day' she had in hand.

— It's awfully difficult, but how on earth can I attend interviews if I can't get time off? I've asked if I could have it without pay, but that only made them more suspicious.

— You'll have to go sick; that's what most people do (said George).

— I suppose so. But I hate telling lies and when I do take time off the others have to do my work between them.

— That's what they would have to do if you were really sick. Anyway that's their problem. After all, it's only once in your life.

— The other thing is that most jobs seem to be in factories. I couldn't possibly work in a factory, George. No-one in our family has ever done that, and being called an 'office machine worker' or 'operative' doesn't help. Linda and Susan were quite shocked when I told them. I do hope the right job turns up soon.

— Have you heard anything from the agencies yet?

— Yes. They've circulated details about me to a lot of firms, but in most cases it's either for a job I don't want or else the firm will consider me for any 'suitable vacancy'. I suppose I should be glad they're prepared to see me but I can't afford to attend more than one or two 'on spec'. Frankly, I'm not very impressed with the agencies. They seem to want just enough information to suit themselves and then get you off their books as soon as possible. One was a bit better, though. The

everything in the store. That would be worth quite a bit to us,
George—10 per cent off furniture and clothes. I thought at
first they were a bit reluctant because I was engaged, but as
they take married women up to 50 I could always go back—as
I told them!

— Well, it's up to you, Christine. But if you're looking for more
money (and that's why you're changing your job, isn't it?) I
should have thought you'd have gone for the job with the
highest salary.

— But you don't understand! What matters is whether I'm
going to like the place and the people—as well as the money.
Surroundings and friends are very important. I saw one of
the girls from school there and they let me talk to her for a
minute. She likes it—and if she does then so shall I!

— I don't see that that follows . . .

— Maybe you don't, but I do. Oh, George, I hope they hurry up
and let me know quickly. I can't bear being kept in suspense.


## Commentary

What can we learn from Christine that is worth bearing in mind
when recruiting people for office work? First, that many young
people are subjective—and often irrational—in their choice of job.
Knowing that a friend is working happily in a similar job may
outweigh possible objections and act as a strong incentive to do
likewise. Every office is in some respects unique and a person's first
reaction to the atmosphere of the office is often a good indication of
whether he or she will settle there.

Secondly, social prejudice runs deep and dies hard. Few
factories today bear any resemblance to the 'dark satanic mills' of
yesteryear. But in the minds of many aspiring young people a
factory is still downgrading no matter how pleasant its environment
may be. However distorted this impression might be, young
potential office staff tend to shun clerical jobs which are inside a
factory. Such prejudices are hard to overcome, but can be dispelled
gradually by letting people see what the factory is really like and by
encouraging employees to introduce their friends.

As conditions in factories improve and as offices become more
like mechanized workshops, the glamour and status of office work is
being steadily eroded. Introducing job titles borrowed from the

shop-floor (eg machine operator) only makes it harder to recruit office staff. Some managers are insensitive to these subtleties and dismiss them as irrelevant; but turning a blind eye to the reality of social prejudice does not mean that it ceases to exist. It is more likely to result in the jobs remaining vacant.

The advent of computers and the mechanization of routine office tasks is demanding new skills and, in many cases, higher scholastic attainments. Industrial offices are in direct competition with the banks and professional firms for these talents. To attract such people to office machine work in large commercial offices is no easy proposition. For some jobs candidates with higher academic qualifications may have to be sought and identified; via employment agencies rather than the Department of Employment; by restyling recruitment advertisements and publishing them in different media; by regrading jobs within the salary scales; and with the help of test batteries, in addition to interviews, at the assessment stage of selection work. Whether or not the long term changes in office work warrant description as 'the office revolution' may be debatable; but their inevitable and far-reaching effects on office recruitment methods should not be ignored.

Many employers still adopt different attitudes towards women assuming, consciously or subconsciously, that a young woman who is engaged or married is unlikely to stay, will act 'irresponsibly' (ie family commitments will come first), that she will be reluctant to relocate or travel, and therefore, investment in training will be largely wasted. However, the turnover among men is frequently as high, if not higher, than among women; men, too, have family commitments. They can be equally 'irresponsible and inflexible". It is, of course, illegal to ask about marriage or family plans at an interview.

Christine's difficulty in attending interviews raises another fundamental problem—that of asking for leave of absence from her present job. The problem is not, of course, peculiar to office staff, but its moral implications rarely receive much attention. Prospective employers can help Christine, and themselves, by a willingness to arrange interviews in the lunch hour and early evening. Unless this is done, some would-be applicants will not be able to attend without being disloyal or dishonest to their present employers. The average employee cannot afford to resign from one job before starting to apply for another, nor is it reasonable to do so. The irresponsible individuals have no compunction about inventing plausible excuses for their short term absences. The more responsible ones face a moral dilemma which industry inflicts upon them.

If Christine Owen lives in your town and is thinking of changing her job, would she apply to your company? What would her impressions be?

  (i) Would she hear favourable comments from her contemporaries?

 (ii) Would she have an immediate opportunity to meet her future boss and see something of the department?

(iii) Would she be interviewed by someone sensitive to aspects such as social status?

(iv) What attitudes would she find towards an 'engaged' woman?

 (v) Through which channels would she have heard of your vacancy?


## The graduate


Graduate recruitment is a perennial nightmare in many companies. It can also be costly and very time-consuming. Employers, students and university appointments boards are all conscious that they have some mutual interests, but find it uncommonly difficult to tune in to the same wavelength. Fewer mistakes would be made if employers accepted the proposition that graduates are likely to be perceptive as well as intelligent. They will probably go to some trouble to find out their own market value and to make diligent enquiries about any company which invites them to join its ranks. Their attitudes will be conditioned by what they see when visiting a firm as well as by what they read from the firm's handouts and brochures. Undergraduates talk amongst themselves about career prospects and each common room has its equivalent of a consumers' guide which, although unwritten, sets out to answer the question *which employer?* At times 'good' undergraduates can count on receiving two offers for every three applications they make, there is more than a suspicion that it is they who choose the employer rather than the other way round. Charles Newton was able to do this—and he is certainly not alone in that respect.

Charles Newton's father had no doubt that his son was 'a chip off the old block' and should make his career in export sales. Charles was inclined to agree. His father, a director of British Exporters Ltd, had fixed him up with vacation jobs which had given him a chance to see something of export sales activities in several different companies. In this respect, Newton had the edge on most of his contemporaries at his university. Their vacations had been spent doing mundane clerical and manual jobs. They had found the cash useful—but the experience had put them off industry for life. Newton saw in export sales an opportunity to use his knowledge of modern languages, in which his tutor had said that he should get a second. He also reckoned that he would find individual responsibility, personal freedom and good prospects of promotion. Now in his final year at university, he availed himself of a talk with the assistant secretary of the appointments board. Newton wanted to confirm his own impressions and to be put in touch with the right sort of companies. Having looked down a long list of firms who said they wanted arts graduates, Newton eliminated some of them on the spot. The common room gossip had forewarned him that these were unattractive. The discussion produced a shortlist of four firms which sounded interesting. Newton duly glanced at their brochures (some were out of date) and rummaged among the file copies of company reports. Browsing again through the *The Directory of Opportunities for Graduates*, his eye was struck by International Electricals Ltd. He added its name to his shopping list. On Newton's behalf, the assistant secretary wrote to the personnel manager of all five companies and he was duly invited to meet the company's representatives. As the appointments board had only limited interviewing accommodation to offer, several companies suggested meeting for a preliminary discussion at a hotel in January 'when our university recruiting team will be visiting your area'. Newton consulted the common room for guidance on protocol.

— *You'll have to wear your dark lounge suit, college tie and polish your shoes—and get your hair cut. Be as conventional as you can. Don't forget to have some questions ready to ask them.*

— *Questions?*

— *Anything they like talking about. Their overseas trade position, their training scheme, what they would expect you to be doing in five years' time: that sort of thing. Careful about salaries: leave that until last, then raise it in a casual way—they like that. Tell them how hard you have worked (not too hard mind, or they will think you are dim) and how you struck a good balance between work and pleasure. You have benefited as widely as possible from university life and like meeting people from other countries—but for heaven's sake tone down the parties and boozing side. Good luck. Don't let them talk you into making a decision on the spot. Go and have a look at the place before committing yourself, and make sure the salary is in writing before you accept the job.*

Heeding these words of worldly wisdom, Newton duly presented himself for the preliminary interviews. There was little to choose between them. A typical one ran rather like this. It lasted about 20 minutes and there were two interviewers.

— Ah, come in, come in. You must be—let me see now— Charles Percival Strang-Newton.

(Newton winced. Why had his parents strung his name out like that. Didn't sound right in the industrial context).

— Yes, that's right.

— Good, good. Sit down won't you.

(Casual eyes watched his every movement).

— Well now. My name is Arkwright—not the inventor of the engine, you know—ha, ha. And this is my colleague, Sally Anderson. She is assistant chief technical officer in charge of all apprentice training and recruitment. I'm from personnel.

— How do you do.

— How do you do. Now then, could you tell us all about yourself?

— Well—er yes, but what do you want to know?

— What you have done in life so far—your home, schools, exams, what you're doing here and so on.

(Newton outlined his career to date.)

— Good, good. Are you expecting to get a good degree?

— My tutor says I should get an upper second.

— Good, and what do you think?

— I hope she's right.

— Ha, ha. And so do we! so do we!

— About how long do you work daily?

— About average, I suppose.

— Good. And what do you think you have got out of your time here—other than a degree?

— I've had a chance to meet all sorts of people.

— *All* sorts of people?

— Yes, you know, people from all over the world.

— That's fine, fine. Now what do you want to do when you graduate?

— I had thought about export sales.

— Any particular product?

— No, not really.

— You would have to learn all about it of course.

— Of course.

— You wouldn't mind that?

— I should like to.

— That's fine, fine.

  Any questions, Sally?

— No, I don't think so.

— Well now, Mr—er—Strang-Newton, have you any questions you'd like to ask us?

— Yes, one or two if I may. What is your export trading position?

— I'm glad you asked that question.

  (Mr Arkwright expanded on this at length.)

— Any other questions?

— Yes, could you please tell me a little about your training scheme?

  (Ms Anderson did so at length.)

— One final question: could you give me a general idea of what my salary progression would be likely to be?

— Ah, yes, salary.

  (Long pause while he ferreted among some papers.)

— Yes, salary—here we are. Arts graduate, second class honours: starting salary—£6,500. That's about the market rate, isn't it?

  (It *was* two years ago, Newton thought, remembering the common room discussion.)

— Just a nominal one you know, while you're under training. And after that—well, it's up to you.

— I see. What might I be earning by the time I am 30?
— Oh, that's very hard to say. Depends on how you progress.
  But we aim to keep all salaries under review and you'll have
  to leave that to us.
  Isn't that right, Sally?
— Yes, that's right.
— Any more questions?
  (He looked at his watch rather obviously.)
— I don't think so.
— Good. Well the next stage will be for you to come and see us
  during your Easter vacation, when we can have a better look
  at you and we'll see where we go from there. Will you be free
  on 14 April?
— (Newton consulted his diary.) Yes.
— Good. Well we'll write to confirm it. Oh, and perhaps you
  would fill in this application form and send it on to us in the
  meantime.
  Good morning.
— Good morning.
  "All running to form" (he later reported to his friends).
  Seems I shall be busy during the Easter vac!
      At Easter Newton went the rounds. The procedure varied a
bit, some companies making a bit of a splash (a room at the best
hotel: lunch in the board room, taxi to the station, first class rail
fare. "Rather pleasant but quite unnecessary", thought Newton.
"Bet they're making a good profit.") Others gave him a glimpse of
later reality (accommodation at local boarding house where other
trainees were staying, and lunch in the canteen). "A bit Spartan",
he thought. "Don't take much trouble over their recruitment—
canteen's as bad as the refectory. Still, I know what I'd be letting
myself in for: with a vengeance.")
      The selection procedures varied from another and longer
interview with the recruiting officer plus a chat with one of the
managers, to a two-day affair with tests and group discussion as
well as the inevitable interviews. He told his friends about it later.

— *We were herded together in a waiting room and introduced to the
  others. After a while a character came in, told us what we had let
  ourselves in for and sorted out our expenses—no chance of
  making anything there!! Then they gave us some intelligence*

tests—none of them said why. I should have thought that a degree was sufficient indication, anyway. After that, we had coffee with the interviewing panel—interesting to see how they reacted to each other. One chap was even running down his own company in our hearing: that one was out! The next torture rack was the discussion group. We all sat in a circle pretending to be nice and friendly, and they gave us some inane subjects to discuss. "What factors should be taken into consideration when choosing where to go for a holiday?" was one: couldn't be bothered with that. And another "Is nationalization of all major industries inevitable?" I ask you, at a nationalized industry! We all willingly gave the acceptable answers. Another was something about analysing our reasons for failing to export enough and saying how we might do something about it. Quite interesting that one, but had to be cautious—thought they bristled a bit when I said trading on a good name was out. Don't think I'd go there. Don't know what they reckon they learned about us—how much we knew about the subject, I suppose—must ask one of the psychology students some day.

Then we had the interviews. Usually longish affairs going over every detail of your life. Most of them don't so much as ask a by your leave, before they want to know whether your father still lives with your mother. Damned cheek. One woman handled it very well though—can't think why the others didn't do the same. She said something like "I've had a good look at your application form and the notes I made when we met at the Salisbury Hotel, so I don't want to go over that ground again. (Wish the rest had bothered to do so: one chap asked me which university I was at and it was staring him in the face!) She went on—now I want to get to know a bit about you as a person, the things you're really looking for in life, how far you're hoping to go, what is going to be important to you when choosing your job. The more you can tell me, the better I shall be able to see whether we have the right job for you. Take your time: I've set aside about three-quarters of an hour for our chat." I liked that—told her a bit more than I should have, I expect, but she seemed really interested and, well, I suppose the more they know about you the better they can fix you up.

The ones that really got me down were those who obviously had no idea what they were going to do with you. Take International

*Electricals Ltd. So far as I could see, they want arts graduates because their engineers can't speak foreign languages, but they haven't a clue what to do with them when they've got them. Waffled vaguely about seeing something of manufacture and home sales before going on the export side in about five years' time—and had no idea how she was going to train me. We'll sort that out when you get here—depending on your progress"—she called it 'a flexible training scheme'. If you ask me, it was an excuse and I doubt if they've ever had an arts graduate before. Won't entrust them with my future, I can tell you. Would you? By contrast, take the shoe firm and the oil company I saw: no vagueness there, I'm not saying that I liked—or agreed with— all their ideas, but at least they've been training graduates for years and could give a straight answer to your questions.*

*I decided on Oil International finally: knew what they were doing and where they were going. Took some trouble over their recruitment and employed people in the personnel department who knew their job and interviewed you properly. Salary's good too—not outstanding—but fair, and prospects are good. Met someone there who was here three or four years ago: nice chap—doing quite well, too. Think I could fit in there and make the most of myself. Better see about getting a decent degree now, I suppose.*

## Commentary

Few graduates have any detailed knowledge of industry or of the choices open to them. They realize that they still have a lot to learn and, on the whole, look to their first employer to provide it. Within reason they are prepared to accept a company's claims for its training arrangements. But a graduate is likely to become suspicious if a company fails to explain in simple language why it wants graduates and what it intends doing with them now and in the future. Their suspicions are often justified. A common danger signal is the bland claim 'our training arrangements are designed to meet the particular requirements of each individual'. It is far more convincing to produce one or two sample training programmes or to outline the career patterns of several previous trainees. And if the company has a satisfied graduate trainee, why not get him or her to help with the recruitment programme? Their reports may be worth hearing too!

The selection procedures must be appropriate and they must be explained. Intelligence tests will reveal more than 'enough ability to obtain a degree', if they are administered and interpreted by a trained person—so why not say so? Group procedures, too, need explanation before they are inflicted on a bunch of people who are not in a position to protest. The preliminary interview does little more than give each party a chance to form a general impression of the other. The fuller interview which comes later should be prefaced by an explanation of its purpose. The interviewer should ensure that the graduate knows what is expected and is motivated to respond fully. Otherwise, the interview can be fraught with misunderstanding. A graduate usually lives a full life and is liable to hold forth on subjects which the interviewer does not wish to pursue, unless given firm guidance from an interviewer who is familiar with the undergraduate way of life.

Until recently, the role of many appointments boards has been mainly that of liaison between the faculty, student and the prospective employer. The better informed a board is about a company, the more likely is it that the board will be able to help. The usual glossy brochure is less informative than would be the career patterns of one or two successful graduate trainees. The influence of faculty staff should not be underestimated, particularly in the scientific and technological fields. Some students rely wholly on their advice—and personal contacts—instead of registering with the appointments boards. They would not be human if they did not steer their protégés towards companies which they know from their personal knowledge to have significant research or design facilities and to have scientific aims akin to their own.

There is some substance in the criticism that companies do not always know why they are recruiting graduates or what they are going to do with them once they have got them. This may be apparent to the graduates, even at the preliminary interview stage; and it is better that they should find out during the selection process, rather than discover it after they have been with the company for three months. At least they will be spared the frustration which comes from boredom, even though the prospective employers are frustrated in their short term and short sighted recruitment aims. The appointments boards have the unenviable task of acting as honest broker between two parties who may not have defined clearly what they have to offer, and who find it hard to communicate with each other. Research studies suggest that the typical graduate would like her/his first job to be one which:

(a) enables her to make direct use of her degree knowledge;
(b) offers opportunities for early responsibility and freedom of action;
(c) enables him to prove himself by making a recognizable contribution to the enterprise;
(d) keeps open the possibility of moving to different work, partly to broaden her experience, and partly as insurance in case her own interests should change after exposure to an environment which is at present unknown to her.

These aspirations do not seem unreasonable, nor are they incompatible with the reasons given by companies for recruiting graduates. These often include, with varying emphasis: the intake of potential managers from whose ranks the company's future leaders are expected to emerge; the topping up of the professional sector of its labour force; and the acquisition of a few of the more able people of each generation, in order that the company will be equipped to keep pace with new developments in the future. Not all graduates can rise to the top in industry; not all of them have the talent and ambition to do so. The post war years saw many mistakes in recruitment through excessive zeal on the part of employers and reliance on the naïve assumption that a university degree was itself a passport to success in industry. Both employers and graduates have become somewhat disenchanted as a result. In the national interest, it is worth going to a good deal of trouble to ensure that graduates are constructively engaged in tasks which they can do well. The country can ill-afford to have some of its best brains misapplied or underemployed.

Let us go back for a moment to Charles Newton and assume that he is due to be interviewed by your company tomorrow:

(i) Are you sure that the work demands a university education or could it be performed satisfactorily by a young person with appropriate A levels and three years' practical experience?
(ii) Have you planned how you will train the graduate and keep him/her constructively employed?
(iii) Would she/he have a predictable avenue of promotion or might he/she become frustrated and leave?

(iv) What proportion of the graduates recruited by your company have left within three years of engagement? Within five years?

(v) Would Charles Newton be convinced by your answers to these questions?

(vi) Would he be right to be convinced?

## The manager

Personnel managers do not often recruit and select other personnel managers. Paradoxical as it may seem, that is one reason for asking Joan Beresford, who is 'one of us', to describe how she changed her job. She found herself for a little while on the other side of the interviewer's desk. The typical reader of this publication will only do so three or four times during the whole of his or her working life. Perhaps that explains why so many mistakes are made when conducting recruitment and selection work for managerial appointments. At this level, it is particularly necessary to anticipate what the would-be-candidate will be looking for—and to plan every step of the recruitment campaign with this in mind. It is worth considering what we ourselves might regard as important when changing jobs; and to contemplate what our reactions, as candidates, might be to the recruitment activities of our own firm. Some lessons can be learnt which have general relevance to the filling of other managerial positions.

21 October 1985

Dear Jack,

Many thanks for acting as one of my referees. I've accepted the job, and shall be starting there next month. Hope you didn't have to perjure yourself too much—I'll buy you a large whisky next time we meet! Sorry I wasn't able to go into details on the telephone, but I'm very pleased with the way things finally turned out. I thought you might be amused to know the background, so I'm enclosing some of the 'documents in the case'. Let me have them back eventually—I should love to have your comments.

I had been thinking of making a move for some time, but I didn't want the word to get around. In many ways I have been very happy here, but gradually became bored with running a department which somebody else had set up in a firm which is thoroughly sold on the value of good personnel management. Of course, some people would say I'm crazy to move! But I want a job with some challenge in it, a chance to build up something from scratch and to try out some of my own ideas.

I read a good many advertisements before I found anything that sounded suitable. Really, some of those advertisements! They tell you virtually nothing about the company or the size of the job. As for salary—conspicuous by its absence in most cases. I must say, it made me take a new look at our own advertisements; it's salutary to see things from the other side of the fence occasionally. Well, to cut a long story short, two jobs caught my eye—one advertised by a firm of consultants and the other was in a personnel magazine. They appeared at about the same time and I decided to have a go at both.

The consultants asked me to meet their Mr Connell who was handling the assignment. He briefed me on the company, giving me a chance to get the feel of the total job situation, including possible snags. He'd obviously studied my application form pretty carefully, because he soon got down to business. Incidentally, have you seen one of their application forms? It concentrates on the important things, with a final section which is a sort of autobiography, self-analysis and the opportunity to sell yourself. It takes some filling in, but gives you a chance to do yourself justice—and presumably helps them with their initial sifting.

The interview lasted $1\frac{1}{4}$ hours so he had plenty of time to get to the bottom of things and give me a chance to ask questions. I wish I had time to interview in depth like that. Going home on the train, I jotted down what I could remember of one part and I'm enclosing it with this letter in case you're interested.

Well, he put me on the short list and I agreed to let my name go forward. The company ran a group selection at their head office. I was quite keen by the time I arrived and was looking forward to seeing some of the directors. But what a fiasco! I should think they made nearly every mistake in the book. These group selections aren't always a good idea and most of us felt a little uncomfortable. Two people in the short list knew each other, for example, and were clearly embarrassed. They tried to be super-efficient, keeping us on the go all the time. We had tests, including a personality one, an open discussion, board interviews, and finally a group exercise! It was obvious that they had never run one of these before, and the topics were badly chosen and badly introduced. The board interview was a gem! It would have been funny, if the situation hadn't meant so much. Five directors lined themselves up on the other side of a massive board room table and within ten minutes they were all talking at once. I did my best—but it wasn't long before they didn't need me at all! Needless to say, I wrote them a note as soon as I got home and withdrew. I hadn't realized before how dismally a firm of consultants can be let down by their clients later. In all fairness, they did warn me, but I didn't think that any board of directors would be quite so ham-fisted, these days!

The other firm—Easdale's—was as different as chalk from cheese. Their letters were almost pure Victoriana! Masses of medallions, heavily embossed parchment paper. I'm enclosing the one inviting me to the interview: needless to say, they gave me hardly any notice and coincided with my visit to France— which I had already told him about. Poor Ms Higgins! She changed the date, of course, amid profuse apologies.

I quite enjoyed my 'interview' with her—she's retiring at Christmas—a nice old welfare type who hasn't a clue about modern personnel practice. Her arrangements for expenses were equally Victorian, and when I pointed this out you'd have thought she had to pay me out of her own pocket! She didn't really interview me at all—just let me ask questions and see the place, which suited me very well. Her secretary seemed pretty efficient and the department has a useful nucleus of established routines, records and procedures.

Afterwards I was interviewed by two of the directors. It's an old family firm which has just been handed over to the next generation. Jack Easdale, the new managing director, is in his thirties, Cambridge and Harvard, and he certainly knows where he's going. It's not exclusively family and there's a chance of a seat on the board in a couple of years. I was rather surprised that they allowed Alison Higgins to handle the initial interviews, but the managing director said he wanted any newcomer to have a clear picture of the present position—and didn't want to hurt Alison's feelings.

Anyway, we got on very well together and I've now accepted the job. It's a gamble, I know, but it should give me plenty to do for quite a time. Of course, it will mean moving away from London, but I'll be back in the country at last, and there's an excellent repertory theatre about 10 miles away. And it will be wonderful to escape commuting every day!

Kindest regards,<br>Joan

*Consultants' advertisement*

---

# Group Personnel Manager

### *Food Industry*

for a group with 5 factories in S London, E Anglia, Yorkshire and SW Scotland employing about 4,000 people. This is a new appointment based at Head Office in London.

The Group Personnel Manager will be responsible to the Managing Director. He/she will advise the Board on all personnel matters, initiate and introduce progressive personnel techniques and assist all managers to deal effectively with their personnel problems.

Candidates, men or women, age 35 to 45, should be graduates, preferably members of the IPM, and must be trained and qualified personnel specialists now holding a senior appointment in a group operating sophisticated personnel techniques. Starting salary £30,000+ with prospects of directorship. Non-contributory pension scheme.

Please write to A B Connell, quoting P 3456 and stating how each requirement is met.

*Advertisement from personnel magazine*

# Group Personnel Manager

*Company*    The Easdale Textile Company Ltd has seven factories in Yorkshire and Lancashire employing over 5,000.

*Job*    The Group Personnel Manager will take over from the Personnel Superintendent who is due to retire at the end of the year. The personnel department (est. 1943) covers recruitment, welfare and sports facilities, pensions and sickness benefits, industrial relations and general personnel services. The Group Personnel Manager's immediate job will be to review personnel policies and practices and to extend the service throughout the entire group. Staff for the department includes five personnel officers. Canteens, security and cleaners all report through their departmental heads to the Group Personnel Manager.

*Remuneration*    Starting salary subject to negotiation but not less than £25,000 pa plus profit sharing. Life assurance scheme and other benefits including share option scheme.

*Applicants*    Should have a university degree and preferably have attended a one year full time course in personnel management. Should have at least ten years' experience of personnel work. Personal qualities are important.

*To apply*    Write in the first instance to Ms A. Higgins marking the envelope 'Private and Confidential.'

THE EASEDALE TEXTILE CO LTD
BRADFORD, YORKS.

*Letter from Easedale Textile Co Ltd*

2 August 1985

Dear Ms Beresford,

Further to our communication of 26 July, in which we acknowledged yours of the 21st instance, we have much pleasure in inviting you to attend for interview at 2 30 on Thursday next, 8 August. We enclose a voucher for your return rail fare; a subsistance allowance will be paid according to the enclosed schedule.

I look forward to the pleasure of making your acquaintance.

Yours truly,

A HIGGINS
*Personnel Superintendent*

*Extract from consultant's interview*

— Now, Ms Beresford, would you tell me about the range of your personnel experience, starting with what led you into personnel work in the first place. As fully as you like, I won't interrupt unless I'm not clear on something.

— Right! I first thought about going into personnel work during my final year at university when I made arrangements to attend the one-year course. I didn't know much about it then, but it seemed as if it might be an interesting field to work in; a developing field that should give considerable scope for development. These ideas were confirmed later, although some of my idealism has now gone and I think I see things rather more realistically. I don't think my motives were 'do gooding', although there was probably a small element of that at the time. I still believe that management is only just beginning to learn how best to organize itself so that it gets the full cooperation of its employees, both individually and collectively. Do you follow me?

— Yes, I understand perfectly.

— Well, I got my first job through the advice of my tutor. (Here I outlined my training and duties in my first appointment.)

— Looking back, do you think that your training might have been improved in any way?

— Oh yes, undoubtedly. The firm had had few people like myself and didn't quite know how to use us.

— Can you be more specific? In what ways did the training fall down?

— Over such things as guiding me so that I made the most of my time in a department. My training supervisor was a good man, but he didn't know enough, I fancy, either about personnel work or my needs, and so it amounted to learning by exposure, rather than giving me an aspect—or several aspects—to investigate, and then report back and discuss them. Also, my one-year course had given me a theoretical appreciation of personnel work, but now I had to see things through the other end of the telescope, as it were. It was a valuable background but at the time it was difficult to make the two compatible.

— How would you overcome these problems, if you were running such a course yourself Ms Beresford?

— I'd make a number of changes. For a start, I should want to know—as clearly as possible—what job trainees are likely to be given at the end of the training period. I suppose that sounds obvious, but it needs emphasizing. Also, I would give them an early taste of the ultimate job, if possible, so that they get an overall impression of what is involved and, at the same time, realizes where their weaknesses lie, what experience is needed to get and so on. I think you need to have a clear picture of all the requirements an individual has, and to plan the course accordingly. If the person in question is a graduate, he or she will have been taught to examine problems from first principles, to subject them to detailed analysis and then to weigh other people's interpretations and, finally, to make up his or her own mind, arguing from evidence available. I would try to enable graduates to apply their trained minds to the industrial situation, giving as much information as can be digested, so that as problems are examined, they realize their own deficiencies. Then, special periods of attachment would be arranged, to fill in the gaps and so on. Lastly, when the graduate had acquired a fairly comprehensive picture of the total personnel function and of its problems, we could examine together how best to match company demands with his or her own interests and preferences.

— That's fine. When referrring to your first job on your

application form, you mentioned an interest in shift work. Could you tell me a little more about this?


## Commentary

Joan Beresford is not a model personnel manager. Nor would she think of herself as a model candidate, but a lot can be learned from her experience of changing her job. At executive level, the selection process is most obviously a two-way affair with a series of judgements and decisions being made by both parties. The candidate goes through a deliberate process of assessing the job and the company at each stage and she consciously weighs up whether she is sufficiently interested to proceed further. Her mental processes run parallel to whether to accept the job when an offer is made; and on her decision depends the outcome of all the recruiter's efforts. It is important, therefore, to understand what is likely to influence her favourably or unfavourably at each stage of the recruitment and selection procedure.

First, she is unlikely to be out of work. Secondly, she is not prepared to prejudice her present job or embarrass her employer by allowing it to become known that she is looking for another job. Indeed, she may not be actively doing so. More frequently she will be keeping her eyes open in case an attractive opportunity comes along, but without having made a firm decision about when or even whether she will move to another company. However, she is likely to have a fairly clear view of what might interest her. The next appointment she takes must seem to be a positive step towards the fulfilment of her career ambitions and must be free of what she regards as limitations in her present job.

Advertisements are scrutinized thoughtfully by Joan Beresford (and by most other executives). She will be disinclined to apply unless she sees some *prima facie* evidence that the advertised appointment might, on balance, represent an improvement over her present one. Her eyes are on the future as well as on the present. Before she will put herself forward as a candidate, she wants to feel reasonably assured that the job is one which she would like to have. It is the recruiter's task to supply Joan Beresford, as far as possible, with the desired information and to prompt her to take the first step by putting her in the right frame of mind. Once again, the starting point must be the job/person specification; and, in addition, the recruiter must consider how much background information about the company should be conveyed in order to present a clear picture of the size and scope of that job and of the context in which it is to be performed. The draft advertisement (assuming that the job is to be advertised) must be double-checked by the recruiter before it is released for publication. It will certainly be taken to pieces by the Joan Beresfords at whom it is being directed. The job title may not be suitable for the advertisement heading if it fails to convey accurately to an outsider the real nature of the work and the appropriate level of seniority. It should not be taken for granted that is will do so, since job titles can be notoriously misleading. The job dimensions can be indicated by factual references to, for example, the number of employees, proposed salary for the appointment, company turnover and growth rate etc. The advertisement should contain some such measurements to enable the potential candidate to judge whether the job is bigger or smaller than the job he or she is already doing. Salary is, of course, one such measurement but it is not the only relevant one nor is it the only motivating factor. However, the reader who is left with no clue about whether the job will carry a higher or lower salary than he or she is currently receiving may hesitate to apply. If the salary is published it must be realistically in line with the current market value for the type of candidate being sought. The company which recruits infrequently at management level may be wide of the mark, unless its salary structure is attuned sensitively to outside salary trends. Consultants are better placed in this respect because of their up to date knowledge of prevailing salaries and they can withhold the client's identity at the advertising stage, if it cannot be published safely in conjunction with the salary which is to be offered.

Managerial candidates also want to be assured explicitly that no information will be disclosed about any applications they make. Executives are more willing than is sometimes supposed to complete application forms provided that the questions asked are relevant and they have already been told enough about the job to be seriously interested in finding out more. In doing so, they like to feel that their application forms do full justice to what they can offer as individuals and an open-ended autobiographical section goes some way towards meeting that need, as well as providing the selector with useful clues about the candidates' attitudes and personal backgrounds. On the other hand many executives today have a well prepared curriculum vitae which not only gives the future 'track record' and personal details but also reveals what the individual considers to be of significance. If carefully studied a curriculum vitae can yield as much information—or more—than an application form but it is not so easy to compare the candidates point for point.

At the interview, the candidate will expect to be given ample opportunity to ask questions. Much can be learned from the questions asked and from the way they are put; and failure to raise certain points may also be significant. Typically, each interview will last for an hour or longer and the candidate will usually have to undergo more than one. The selector is not only concerned with finding out what the candidate knows, but also with probing the reasons for present attitudes and past behaviour. It is unreasonable to expect executives to turn up for interview at the drop of a hat. They have forward commitments in their present jobs and cannot cancel meetings or business engagements at short notice. Unless given at least 10 days' notice, they may find it difficult to attend.

The candidate will form his or her own impression of the interviewer. The skilled interviewer will earn respect, as well as finding out much more about the candidate. When dealing with candidates for senior positions, the untrained interviewer, relying on impromptu remarks and subjective conclusions, is at a marked disadvantage and can be fooled by a candidate who knows much more about the interview situation than he or she does. Joan Beresford was given a rough ride in the first job for which she was considered and she had good reaon to withdraw her application. Few employers make so many mistakes at the same time—but it is surprising how many are made. Some boards of directors seem fond of forming themselves into interviewing panels and fail to see the clumsy and forbidding picture of themselves which they present to the shortlisted executives. Even the most ardent applicants might be daunted by the curious, and often atypical scenes enacted before them. Companies sometimes forget in their enthusiasm to try out modern selection techniques that group selection programmes require careful and skilful planning; and even then, an embarrassing situation can arise if the candidates are known to each other.

Not infrequently, an executive will have to move house before accepting another job and will not rush into this without weighing carefully all the implications. A partner's attitude and preferences can tip the balance. The risk of disrupting children's education can be a major obstacle. Before accepting the offer of an appointment, the successful candidate will weigh many factors in the balance including the social and financial costs of moving. Increased salary can be a powerful inducement—but the main attraction will often centre on the immediate challenge presented by the job and by the future prospects it offers. Candidates for managerial appointments are discriminating in the comparisons they make between one job and another. It is to the longer term advantage of the prospective employer, as well as themselves, that they should know about and accept the possible snags before tackling a new job rather than discover them afterwards.

Joan Beresford, as our *alter ego*, can now be allowed to retire gracefully from the limelight, but we should not forget how we might have reacted had we been in her shoes. Recall for a moment the most recent occasion on which your company sought to fill an executive appointment and consider how things looked from the viewpoint of an intelligent and experienced candidate. What impressions of your company were created by:

  (i) the wording and layout of the advertisement?
 (ii) the style of correspondence and application form?
(iii) the professional skill of the interviewer?
 (iv) the organization of the short list procedures?
  (v) the presence of your managerial colleagues and by their informal conversations over lunch?

Was the job filled—in spite of the quite unnecessary hazards which existed?

# 3
# Third stage—assessing the candidate

Earlier chapters have emphasized that recruitment and selection work should be thought of as a matching process. This concept is so fundamental that we make no apology for repeating it. Having assessed the demands of the job, we know what attributes we are looking for and we possess in the person specification a yardstick against which we can assess the suitability of the candidate. The next practical step is to decide therefore the methods by which we shall recognize the presence or absence in individual candidates of the attributes we are seeking. Quite simply, we are seeking to obtain, analyse and interpret information about people. In doing so, our immediate aim is to narrow the field of candidates by progressively eliminating those who do not measure up to our person specification. As a secondary aim, we may wish to see whether any of those about to be eliminated would merit consideration for a different job; this is done by subsequently comparing them against the different yardstick for that other job.

Matching implies that candidate requirements which can be measured have been identified in the job and that we know how to measure people in terms of those attributes. Tools and techniques which go a long way towards doing this have been developed during the past 50 years, but they are far from perfect. They are of little use if applied by an unskilled person; nor can satisfactory results be expected if they are applied slavishly to every candidate for every job. All assessment techniques presuppose competence on the part of the user, and that competence comes only from training and practical experience. This is true especially of the most commonly used technique of all; the interview. It is a curious fact that almost everyone prides themselves on being good judges of people. Only bitter personal disappointment seems capable of destroying this self-deception; any reasonable foundation for it disappeared half a century ago, when classic research studies exposed it as a myth.

Demonstrably, some people are capable of becoming more proficient than others at selection work, thus the assessor needs to have been carefully selected. The role of an interviewer demands sensitivity to the process of human interaction, and adaptability to each individual interviewed. We require sympathy and, at the same time, objectivity in order to weigh up a complex range of evidence and reach a firm conclusion. These requirements alone, and there are others, should be enough to dispel the illusion that we are all endowed with a natural gift for picking good employees. Even if such innate talent were universal, it would still not be sufficient. By their nature, other techniques of assessment obviously call for specific training before they can be used at all. The selector has to exercise acquired skill and discretion in applying them, since their value varies considerably according to the type of candidate being assessed. In particular, their use depends on their acceptability to the candidate and this, too, varies with age and with type of occupation.

The selection techniques used most widely in industry at present are:

  (i) the application form

  (ii) the interview

 (iii) group selection methods

 (iv) psychological tests

Each is discussed in some detail later in this chapter and the table (pp 106–7) gives a general indication of the points to bear in mind when considering their possible use. As a guide, the appropriateness of these four techniques has been summarized in relation to half a dozen different categories of potential candidates. The range of techniques available to be used for a particular job depends, in the first place, on the professional competence of the selector. Within that range, the selector's judgement about the combination of techniques to be used will take into account:

  (a) the attributes to be assessed and the degree of accuracy required

  (b) type and level of appointment

  (c) age distribution of candidates

  (d) probable acceptability of the different methods

  (e) time available

  (f) comparative costs

As with any skilled worker, the selectors must know when to

# The Principal Assessment Techniques
## A general guide to their use

| Types of Candidate | Application Form | Initial Interview | Psychological Tests | Group Discussion |
| --- | --- | --- | --- | --- |
| 1 School leavers (and aged up to 18) | Valuable. Should highlight family background and occupations, school performance, examination results (external), hobbies and interests. Keep simple. Avoid asking for irrelevant information. | Need encouragement and sensitive handling, as not used to expressing themselves in a formal situation. Start interview at factual level based on application form, and develop depth questioning later. Expect apparent conflicts in interest and personality patterns at this age. *Typical time: 20–40 mins* | Useful. Can reveal latent as well as actual ability. The general factor 'g' will often 'swamp' other factors; exceptions are spatial and (some) attainment tests. | Only useful with the well above average. (Likely to opt out.) |
| 2 Shop floor operatives, clerical grades | Keep factual and simple. Allow less space for school and plenty of space for work history. Frequency and pattern of job changes is very important. Can omit schooling before age 11, also family traditions, but ask for names of relatives or friends who are employees. | Use a formal, well-structured pattern with direct questions and occasional probes. Explore range of experience and peaks of attainment; also how well they have fitted into other companies. Photographs and display of products make communications easier. *Typical time: 15–30 mins* | Rarely useful or acceptable if aged over 25, except to assess suitability for promotion or retraining. 'Work sample' tests can be valuable if properly devised and conducted, but coordinated dexterity inclined to be highly particularized. | Rarely worth using. |
| 3 Supervisors, senior clerical, senior technicians | Straightforward and easy to complete. Emphasis on school, subsequent academic achievements, range of work experience, responsible roles held at work and outside. | Fairly formal, structured pattern. Probe gaps in application form (if any) and exact nature of experience. Allow at least five minutes for candidate to ask questions. *Typical time: 20–30 mins* | Depends on age and experience. Can be useful when entirely new work to be done, extensive training involved or first supervisory appointment. | For some supervisory posts. Clues to personality factors and management approach likely to be adopted. Guide to breadth of understanding of the problems about to be met. |

| | | | | |
|---|---|---|---|---|
| **4 Graduates** | Carefully designed form should highlight family background, academic and social activities at both schools and university (to show rate of development), participation in university societies. Longer term ambitions may sometimes be more important than shorter term goals. | Flexible pattern and needs delicate handling. Treat as a vocational guidance interview. Encourage them to talk about ambitions and introspections. Relate proven ability and personality to ambitions, in order to judge realistic career pattern. Use open questions and probe. *Typical time: 30–45 mins* | Use general intelligence tests to determine the extent to which they use their ability. This may be masked by (a) over participation in student affairs, (b) choice of subjects to suit a narrow ability, (c) tremendous effort expended to achieve an average result. | Very useful. Guide to personality and ability to apply academic training to real-life problems. |
| **5 Professionally qualified executives** | Design to provide a running outline of home background, schooling qualifications, training and interests. Place emphasis on range and depth of experience (including supervisory roles), self-analysis, and career aims. A good cv may yield all the information needed prior to interview. | Determine the rate and direction of career and personal development by open questions, self-analysis, comparative questions and probing. Pattern of development before 21 particularly important. Exactly similar experience often less important than grasp of principles and good record of application to other tasks. Allow 15 mins for candidate to ask questions. *Typical time: 30–60 mins* | Not always acceptable. Useful, particularly if in doubt about train-ability or administrative ability when 'g' tests coupled with verbal (v:ed) tests can provide additional evidence. | Useful and generally acceptable. Guide to strong attitudes, how well likely to fit in, and ability to apply past experience to new problems. |
| **6 Senior managers** | Administer discriminatingly. Cv may be adequate for first-stage screening in many cases. Avoid asking for unnecessary duplication. Candidate resistance to form-filling not as great an obstacle as generally supposed, if handled tactfully. Use same form as 5, occasionally with specific questions added. | Very flexible approach needed. Discussion interspersed with probing, or information about job/company, followed by 'interview', followed by discussion, or rapid appraisal of basic facts (to fill in gaps and get a balanced picture) followed by discussion of experience and aims. *Typical time: 45–75 mins* | Unlikely to be acceptable in some cases although now becoming used more widely. Effective application of intelligence and administrative aptitude can be assessed by 'g' and v:ed tests. Applied intelligence, eg 'critical thinking', and personality tests can reveal quality of judgement and perceived personality traits. | Sometimes not acceptable, as candidates may fear face to face confrontation with others could jeopardize their present positions. Information sessions, individual or group, may yield sociometric or inter-action information not available in normal interview. |

use each tool, how to apply it and what its inherent strengths and limitations are. To take the analogy further, we should also consider the degree of finish required, since this influences our choice of a coarse or a fine selection device at each stage of the process.

## i  Application forms

Assessment does not start with the interview. For many jobs it is perfectly possible, and indeed sometimes essential, to eliminate the majority of the applicants without even interviewing them at all. In carrying out these preliminary stages of assessment, the selector relies largely on documentary evidence.

Initial letters of application vary widely in the amount of relevant information they contain. Much depends on how the advertisement itself was phrased. If the job was described fairly fully and the candidate requirements were stated in specific terms, the resultant letters of application will contain correspondingly more factual information about the candidate. In such cases, it will often be possible to eliminate between one-third and one-half of the applicants on the strength of their initial letters. By contrast, fewer replies to a woolly advertisement can be eliminated without serious risk of losing potentially worthwhile candidates.

The application form is a basic selection instrument. It is much more valuable than is generally realized. If carefully designed, administered and interpreted, it can provide a wealth of information about a candidate. Conversely, it will prove to be a blunt instrument if these conditions are not fulfilled. Commonly it is misused. Its principal purpose is to ask pertinent questions and elicit relevant information, thus enabling the selector to identify candidates who correspond closely to the person specification. Subsequently, it can serve as a framework around which the interview may be built. Lastly, it can be kept as a record of the employee's background, but this is its least important function.

Unfortunately, an application form is liable to become regarded as part of a standard routine. The procedure tends to obscure the real purpose. There is no point in asking people to fill in a form if their original letters reveal that they fail to meet one or more of the essential requirements of the job. Similarly, there is little point in inviting someone to attend an interview (and to forfeit a day's work in doing so) if careful study of their career record would show that they are unlikely to be suitable for the job. The candidate's time is valuable too.

The application form is therefore basically a method of asking and answering questions by correspondence. The selector should already have a clear idea from the person specification of the criteria by which candidates will be differentiated between. The application form needs to be designed with those criteria in mind. Obviously what the selector wants to know and what the candidate has to say, and is willing to disclose, varies widely according to the type of job to be filled and the age group of the candidates. Seen in these terms, a standard form used for all jobs must be inefficient, since the questions it asks will be irrelevant in some respects to most candidates and the manner and sequence in which they are posed may also be inappropriate. The application form is too valuable a selection instrument to be abused in this way.

In the medium-sized company at least three different versions of the application form will be needed. They will have been especially designed for recruiting different types of employees such as factory and clerical workers; school leavers; and professionally qualified staff and managers. In the larger company, additional variations may be used, according to the range of occupations covered and the scale of recruitment undertaken. When recruiting managerial grades, the application form can be given an even sharper cutting-edge by the addition of several supplementary questions specifically designed to probe the relevance of the candidate's experience. Contrary to popular belief, this improves the form's acceptability to candidates as well as strengthening its technical efficiency, since the relevance of the questions makes it immediately apparent that the form is being administered in an intelligent and purposeful way. Theoretically, the form should always be tailor-made to suit the particular appointments to be filled, but in practice most personnel officers find that three or four basic versions are adequate for most of their recruitment work.

The application form should therefore be administered sensitively and sensibly. We need to bear in mind that many people have a healthy dislike of form-filling and are disinclined to perform this laborious task. A candidate is more likely to complete the application form if a covering letter explains that the initial letter has been read and that the first hurdle has already been surmounted

# THE APPLICATION FORM
A check list of possible coverage

| Subject | | Observations |
|---|---|---|
| Personal particulars | Full name<br>Address (permanent or temporary)<br>Telephone number (home and business)<br>Date of birth<br>Marital status: dependents<br>Height: weight: state of health | |
| Family background | Relations employed by the company<br>Parental occupations<br>Occupations of brothers and sisters | Provides clues to opportunities afforded. For adults, an open-ended question about traditional occupations or professions is preferable. |
| Education—general | Schools attended: name and type<br>Examinations: subjects, grades, dates<br>School offices held<br>Scholarships, prizes | Education since 11 may be sufficient in the case of older applicants |
| —further | College/university: course taken<br>Examinations: subjects, grades, dates<br>Offices held. Extra-curricula activities | |
| Vocational training | Apprenticeship/articles/special training<br>Nature and place of training<br>Professional qualifications: date qualified, present grade of membership<br>Languages: oral, written; degree of fluency | Note whether full time or part time study. |

| | | |
|---|---|---|
| *Employment history* | Complete chronological record of all jobs held with dates<br>Nature and scale of duties, and to whom responsible<br>Name and address of employer<br>Starting and finishing salary<br>Reasons for leaving | Allow sufficient space for present (or last) job to be described more fully. For senior appointments, brief account of significant achievements.<br>Names of referees are better obtained at interview. |
| *Leisure interests* | Hobbies; leisure pursuits<br>Membership of societies; offices held | Establish the range, depth and persistence of what the applicant chooses to do of his/her own free will.<br>A check-list can be provided for completion by school leavers. For senior appointments, can be included in an autobiographical account. |
| *Application* | Type of job sought<br>Date of any previous application<br>When free to start work | |
| *Self-assessment* | Likes and dislikes<br>Special job interests<br>Future aims and ambitions | Should be towards the end of the form.<br>For senior appointments, applicants may be asked to outline how well they meet the requirements set out in the advertisement. |

as forms are not being distributed automatically to everyone who has applied. A common practice is to grade all the initial applications into three categories of unsuitable, possible and interview. The 'unsuitables' are eliminated immediately; the 'possibles' are sent an application form in order to obtain additional evidence about their strengths and weaknesses; whilst the 'interviews' are sent a letter inviting them to an interview and requesting them to return the completed application form when confirming the date of the proposed meeting. The latter procedure is normally used for only the small minority of applicants who conform most closely to the person specification. It reduces the risk that they will lose interest in the appointment, but the application form is still needed as a framework for the interview. It is prudent to carry out a periodic spot-check of the proportion of forms which are in fact completed, as a low ratio may indicate that the form is either badly-constructed or is being administered clumsily.

The table on pp 110–111 may serve as a check-list of possible contents when designing application forms. It should not be regarded as a model, nor is it suggested that every application form should include every item. On the contrary, the essence of a good application form is that it is constructed to suit the particular circumstances, and these vary from job to job and from company to company.

In general, it is better to arrange the items in chronological sequence, but grouping together all aspects of education and training. This is done primarily to simplify the applicant's task, but it also assists the selector by making it easier to identify patterns. Administrative codes and symbols should be kept to the minimum, as they are distracting and may be viewed with suspicion. The layout should allow an adequate amount of space for each item and cater for those with large handwriting. Lines are a great help to many people, especially those unaccustomed to writing. Since the purpose is to elicit relevant information, it is sensible to examine periodically a sample of completed forms in order to check whether the required information is being obtained in a coherent and economical way.

It has been emphasized in earlier chapters that a principal aim is to compare the demands of the job with the candidate's capacities and inclinations by means of a technique such as the seven-point plan or the five-point plan. A good deal of the candidate information to be sought under these systems can be deduced from a well-constructed application form and classified under these seven (or five) headings. The form cannot tell the whole story about the candidate but, carefully interpreted, it can reveal some of the salient features. In particular, it can provide some provisional evidence and clues concerning the applicant's:

biographical data and personal circumstances
career pattern and attainments
powers of self-expression
range and depth of interests
intelligence and special aptitudes
behaviour patterns and preferences

When evaluating a completed application form, it is customary to inspect first the factual sections, in order to see whether the candidate fails to meet any of those *essential* requirements in the person specification. There is nothing to be gained by spending time on a detailed evaluation of the applicants if it is immediately apparent that they lack one of the essential attributes. Perforce, they must be disqualified from further consideration for that particular job, although if other jobs are to be filled as well, this form may repay closer study against different person specifications later.

On completion of this first reading, the applicant can be placed into one of three provisional categories corresponding broadly to unsuitable, possible and probable. The word provisional is used advisedly. A second and more analytical study of the application form is needed in order to select for interview those candidates who correspond most closely to the person specification. The real skill in interpretation and deduction comes into play at this point. A synoptic view of the applicant and of the job now being done will already have been acquired from the first inspection of the application form. The more difficult step is to assess how and why the person concerned has developed in reaching his or her present position. In doing so, we postulate the hypothesis that the pattern of people's previous behaviour can provide some clues to the way they are likely to behave in the future. When assessing older applicants this hypothesis can be relied on with greater assurance than when dealing with younger candidates. It should also be noted that persistent characteristics may be more significant than isolated occurrences.

With practice, much more than appears on the surface can be learnt about applicants by considering how they performed in previous situations, for example at school, at work and in society. The use they have made of opportunities, the handicaps overcome, the extent to which they have proved themselves compatible in different social groupings, are some of the trends and tendencies which may be apparent from past records. Taken together, they can serve as valuable guides when considering jobs for which applications have been received. It is important to bear in mind that even a well-designed application form will not contain all the parts of the jigsaw puzzle we are attempting to piece together. Inevitably there will be some gaps in our knowledge, perhaps vital ones, which remain unfilled. This additional information will have to be gleaned later by tests or by personal interview. Even so, these tentative deductions about the candidate are of considerable value especially as they are made without the interplay of personalities which occurs in the face to face situation of the interview. On the strength of these tentative conclusions some candidates will be eliminated. The remainder will meet the selector who has a clear idea of what else is needed in order to find out about them. An analysis of the application form has enabled the selector to note the areas for which further exploration is necessary and the selector will concentrate on those particular points when planning and conducting interviews. Thus the best use of the time available will be made and interviews will be correspondingly more efficient.

It has become a feature of recent years, perhaps as a result of American influence, that most managers and professional people have a curriculum vitae in their files which they update from time to time. Many of these have been 'professionally' produced and reasonably accurately convey the basic facts about the subject— education, qualifications, career summary—and as such are useful to the selector. However, people are more than the sum total of their parts and the risk is that cvs produced in this way clinically delete individual personality features of the individual, thereby removing the most valuable feature of a self-produced curriculum vitae—a reflection of the writer as conceived by him- or herself. Many recipients so dislike these standard curriculum vitae that they consign them to the waste paper basket; which is a grave injustice to the individual who has paid for advice and help. They are of value in making a quick evaluation and deciding whether to take things further; but in the author's view, no more than that.

## ii  The interview[1]

Interviewing can produce abominable results. It frequently does; but the fault usually lies in the interviewer rather than in the assessment method. Interviewing is an everyday occurrence and is the most widely used assessment technique; it is part of the popular vocabulary; it looks easy, and everyone is inclined to believe they are good at it. Therein lies the danger and the confusion. In practice, many so-called interviews consist of untrained employers talking generalities about jobs they have not analysed to would-be employees about whom they know little, and then deciding whether or not to offer them the job. In such unpropitious circumstances it would indeed be surprising if the predictive value of the interview were anything but poor.

Research studies have demonstrated time and time again that interviewing competence varies enormously, and that some people are very bad at it. Thus it has become fashionable in recent years to disparage the interview. This is no more helpful than condemning the technique of diagnostic examination in the field of medicine, on the grounds that the lay person has difficulty in telling measles from chickenpox! The registered medical practitioner recognizes the difference as a result of relevant training and experience; and the circumstances in which he or she works leave no option but to rely on diagnostic examinations, even though the technique as such depends on human judgement. So it is with the interview in industry. It is a necessary and unavoidable part of the selection process, because it fulfils other functions as well as being a convenient and acceptable method of assessing the candidate. Our efforts therefore should be directed towards improving the

[1]Throughout this publication, the word *interview* relates specifically to the *employment* interview. There are many other circumstances in which a person may be 'interviewed' where the information getting/attitude revelation techniques used in selection interviewing are directly applicable. Most managers 'interview' every day in a wide variety of situations and do not realize that the application of sound interviewing techniques can help them in their day to day work (eg discipline, promotion, salary review, counselling, dismissal, vocational guidance etc).

standards of interviewing, and this is the main theme of this chapter.

## Objectives

The interviewer should have in mind constantly three main objectives. The first, and most obvious, is to establish whether the candidate is suitable for employment and, if so, in what particular job their talents can best be used to mutual advantage.

The second objective is to ensure that the candidates have an accurate picture of the job for which they are being considered. If he or she is a strong contender for the job, it is doubly important to provide a full understanding of what that job entails. It is pointless to gloss over aspects which the interviewer thinks may be unattractive. If, in fact, they are unattractive to that condidate, it is far better to withdraw candidature at the preliminary interview rather than discover them later. A new employee who believes he or she has been misled is unlikely to stay in the job for long.

The third objective is to conduct the interview in such a manner that the candidate feels he or she has had a fair hearing, whether engaged or not. The interview itself assumes a high degree of importance in the minds of the prospective candidates. They are prone to feel acute disappointment if deprived of the opportunity to state their case in person and, if invited to an interview, approach it with high hopes. Their impressions of the company as well as of the job applied for are coloured by the way in which the interview is conducted.

## Some basic faults

Most people who read this publication will readily accept that interviewing calls for skills which have to be learned, can be taught and should be derived from research findings. Even so, few of those same people will have studied the research evidence for and against the interview, and some will be blissfully unaware that its validity as an assessment technique has been repeatedly challenged. Research studies have shown that some of the more prevalent weaknesses can be traced to:

*Brief, unsystematic interviewing* Conclusions are based on hunches rather than on facts, candidates being assigned preconceived classifications without examining all the relevant evidence. "Prejudice is a great time saver—it enables you to form opinions without having to get the facts."

*Inadequate application forms* Vital facts are likely to be missed or misconstrued. The interview may degenerate into an interrrogation through relentless efforts to overcome this deficiency.

*Interviewers unaware of their own limitations* The assessment should be confined to those attributes which the interviewer can measure accurately and reliably. Ill-conceived attempts to isolate and assess such abstract qualities as honesty, conscientiousness, integrity etc may amount to little more than wild guesses. They are notoriously difficult to infer, even where the interviewer has made a careful reconstruction and analysis of the candidate's past behaviour in the context of specific situations.

*Subjective spot-checks* Answers to the interviewer's favourite questions are allowed to assume disproportionate weighting in the final assessment, even though they may not constitute a fair sample of each person's knowledge, or may not correlate with successful performance in that job.

*Failure to establish rapport* This is essentially a matter of communication and mutual trust. The significance of the candidates' words, allusions and social values have to be manifestly understood and respected, before they will confide further facts about themselves to the interviewer.

*Interviewer talks too much* As a general guide, interviewers should be speaking for less than one third of the time. You will usually learn more when listening and the interviewee talking!

*Preparation for an interview*
Before the interview begins, the interviewer should have studied all the available information about the candidate, and particularly the application form, so the task of assessment can be concentrated on fully. By its nature, interviewing is a time consuming process and,

within reason, everything possible should be done to ensure the best use of the time available. A careful examination of what is already recorded will help the selector to plan the interview and to devote the greater part of his time to those aspects which need clarification or amplification.

To advocate that the interview should be planned at all strikes some people as undesirable, whilst others feel compelled to compile a long string of questions or a detailed check-list. Neither extreme is justified. A skeleton plan helps the interviewer to concentrate on observing the candidate and interpreting what is said, instead of frantically wondering what subject to raise next. It helps the interviewer to keep the discussion to the point and avoids the risk of embarrassing pauses. The skeleton plan should not be followed rigidly, but can be modified as the conversation progresses. The interview has to start somewhere; it has to be steered so that it covers the ground indicated in the person specification and it has to be brought tactfully to its close. To do this well requires considerable skill and practice. A detailed check-list can become a strait-jacket, but a brief note of particular facets to be explored and of a few key phrases is invaluable, if not indispensible. A useful technique is to prepare on one sheet of paper a chronological analysis of the application to show concurrent activities—and gaps. Draw up an age scale—present age on the left-hand side. Divide the page vertically into four columns. In column 1 show career landmarks (change of job title, special projects tackled, change of job etc); in the second column education and training courses and results. Use the third column for any other specific activity or achievement (hobby, professional activity, outside work, date married and birth of children, illness etc) and in the final column note inconsistencies, points you are not clear about, for example 'four month gap.; 'why not complete the course—marriage?'; 'sideways move'; apparent drop in salary'; 'took drop to stay in town band?'

This preparation has another value. It facilitates the early establishment of rapport, by demonstrating to the candidate that the information supplied earlier has been studied and found to be of interest. Thus the candidate is encouraged to feel that what is said during the interview will also be considered worthy of interest. The subject of intra-personal communication is discussed more fully later in this chapter. It is relevant here in that the interviewer's preparation has enabled him to give the first clues to the level of communication which can be attained between two people who are strangers to each other. Conversely, rapport will be inhibited if the interviewer's early remarks or questions convey that he has either not read or not remembered what should have been apparent from the candidate's application form.

When an interview programme is being arranged, the times of candidates' arrivals should be carefully spaced so that waiting is kept to the minimum. Apart from considerations of courtesy, candidates are unlikely to do themselves justice if they have become nervous or irritated through being kept waiting. There is another and less altruistic reason. Interviewers are tempted to skimp their preparation if they know they are behind schedule and, in the resultant interview, may not do justice either to the candidate or to themselves.

*The physical setting*

In the normal course of events personnel officers will conduct interviews in their own offices. Some large companies set aside a number of small, quiet rooms furnished informally for this purpose. When a number of candidates from another part of the country are under consideration, it may be advantageous to arrange to see them at a hotel in that district. When doing so, a private room should be reserved. The practice of trying to interview across a luncheon table or in a public lounge is generally to be deplored. The candidate is made unnecessarily tense by the risk of being seen or overheard; and the interviewer will be unable to concentrate properly.

The physical setting has quite an important bearing on the degree of rapport which can be established. An office used for interviewing should be reasonably noise-proof and the furnishings should not be too distracting. Chairs should be so arranged that the interviewer does not appear to be dominating the candidate. With a little forethought, it is seldom necessary for the interviewer to address the candidate across an enormous desk, or from a higher chair, or to have artificial light blazing into the eyes of the guest. Documents which are not needed should be cleared away before the candidate enters the room. There should be complete freedom from telephone calls and other interruptions whilst the interview is in

progress. If notes are to be made, the interviewer must arrange the
seats at a sufficient distance so that the candidate will be unable to
read what is written.

These arrangements are not advocated out of desire to pamper
the candidate: they are essential if the interviewer is to do the job
properly. Concentration is essential. Anyone who believes otherwise has not made a serious study of the subject.

*Conducting the interview*
A delicate balance has to be struck between formality and
friendliness, between clinical examination and casual confidences
entrusted to a sympathetic ear. Solemnity and impressiveness are
regarded by some as being advantages of the selection board
interview, whilst others urge that every interview should be
conducted in a completely informal vein. To the candidate, both
are unnatural and threatening. The interview should be conducted
in an atmosphere which is 'known' and which seems favourable to
both parties. Acknowledge the 'threat' but limit it by conveying to
the candidate that they need not be afraid of admitting their own
shortcomings. Explain, and mean, that everything is confidential.
Be sympathetic and understanding, but always acknowledge the
formal relationship and never take unfair advantage of the
candidate. For this reason it is almost always undesirable to
conduct an employment interview on Christian name terms: false
bonhomie is more threatening than complete formality, because
candidates should know exactly where they stand.

It is fundamental that the candidate should be put at ease on
entering the room. The interviewer's opening remarks are
therefore of paramount importance. They inform the candidate
how he or she is expected to respond and the amount of time set
aside, in order to use the time to the maximum advantage and with
the right degree of emphasis. They set the candidate at ease by
providing an operational framework ("this is what I am aiming to
do"), by motivating a free response and by setting the quiet,
unhurried, sympathetic atmosphere. The candidate has a chance to
get used to the interviewer's voice and to overcome some initial
tension. The introduction should never be stereotyped and should
be adjusted according to the type of person being interviewed.

The interview should start and finish at definite points of

time. There is little time or need for casual chat. The interview should be terminated firmly by telling the candidate when he or she will be informed of the outcome and by a physical movement, such as standing up to help the candidate with his or her coat.

The flow of the discussion is largely in the hands of the interviewer, who must be in control of the situation throughout, however light may be his or her touch. If the interviewer expressed him/herself clearly at the outset, so that the candidate knows in advance what sort of response is expected of him, relevant answers to questions will usually be supplied. If this is not the case, the candidate can soon be directed back to the right lines. Simple praise *("I was most interested in ...")* or blame *("I'd rather we concentrated on ...")* will work wonders on the person who has wandered away from the point.

When learning to interview, some people find it difficult to move from one subject to another and feel compelled to interject "Thank you very much" at the end of each answer. This is quite unnecessary and stresses the undesirable aspects of formality. The good listener will always find a link question from among asides and comments on previous subjects *("You mentioned just now that ... Could you tell me a little more about ...")*. A comparative question will frequently suffice, and, at the same time, introduce a demand for self-insight (*"How did that work compared with ..."*). The interview should not be closed without the candidate being given an opportunity to ask questions and to volunteer information which he or she feels has not been taken adequately into account. This can be achieved quite simply by asking *"Is there anything else you would like to know about this job?"* and by posing a question such as *"Are there any other important aspects you would like to raise?"*

*Communication*
Even experienced interviewers sometimes forget the physical, psychological and emotional difficulties of expressing oneself clearly in an ego-threatening situation. Experience, aims, motives, etc are expressed in words by some people for the first and last time in the interview situation. Personalized memories are hard to express in objective terms and harder still to recall at the drop of a hat. The typical applicant has a vocabulary of about 5,000 words (ie about 10 per cent of the English vocabulary) and so lacks the verbal

equipment to say precisely what he or she means. He or she tries to do so by analogy or by a series of apparently disjointed and often inadequate utterances. This must be allowed for by the interviewer. The candidate must be given time to reply and encouraged to express him/herself freely in revealing the framework of his/her life and thoughts.

If rapport is to be established and held throughout the interview, there must be empathy between the parties concerned. This is communicated through choice of phrase and manner, and particularly by the interviewer's words, emphasis and facial expressions. Communication between human beings is a process involving the senses of sight and sound. The skilled interviewer is aware of the subtleties and shades of meaning that can be communicated, and is sensitive to the differences which age, social environment and intellectual ability can introduce. For examples of good and bad communication see the section headed *Reflections on Recruitment* (page 67).

To a degree which is often underestimated, the interview may impose 'threats' and pressures on the candidate's personality make-up. Status, occupational competence and personal affairs are being exposed to scrutiny. The candidate's livelihood and even the hopes and aspirations of her or his family may rest upon the outcome and the interviewee will naturally be anxious to present him/herself in a favourable light. However, there is a problem. Voluntary disclosure of information may seem like a betrayal of confidences; but non-disclosure may land him or her in a job which he or she cannot do or does not want to do. The skilled interviewer will be sensitive to such pressures. Throughout, the interview will be handled with a delicate touch, giving reassurance after threat and offering the candidates an opportunity to present themselves in their best light before uncovering weaknesses.

*Bias, prejudice and 'halo effect'*
Interviewers can be their own worst enemies. Their efforts towards objectivity will founder if they allow prejudice or bias to distort their judgements. Almost everyone has some prejudices. Though the interviewer will not rid themselves of them completely, they should strive to be aware of them.

Bias and prejudice result partly from the cultural and

environmental influences within which a person has been brought up and partly from the way in which we as individuals have reacted to those background influences. Inevitably, interviewers' own attitudes towards work and towards society reflect their own background to a greater or lesser extent. In order to judge fairly what kind of a person the candidate really is, the interviewer needs to discount personal likes and dislikes and to examine impartially that other person's background and attitudes. Frequently, it will be found that the candidate's background and that of the interviewer have certain features in common, and this can lead to bias on the part of the interviewer; conversely, if the candidate's reactions run counter to the interviewer's, he or she may be biased against that particular candidate. Judgement can be warped in this way without the interviewer being conscious of it.

Prejudices, on the other hand, tend to be associated with persistent attitudes held by the interviewer. Commonly, they are directed towards personal characteristics possessed by other people. Examples are prejudice against people with certain facial features, such as low forehead or a receding chin; against some regional accent, a personal mannerism or aspect of dress; or against those of another race, colour or creed. Such irrational notions are inimical to good interviewing. Though the interviewer may find it impossible to discard prejudices there should be an awareness of their existence and allowance should be made for them in any final assessment. The great danger in bias and prejudice is that they lead to unfair discrimination. Much has been said and written about various forms of discrimination; sexual, racial and colour discrimination can now be challenged at industrial tribunals and penalties will be awarded for infringement. Positive discrimination against the trend is sometimes tolerated, eg in favour of an ethnic minority, and one suspects that a few organizations have swung too far in the other extreme to avoid the stigma of such a charge. The fact remains, however, that most of us nurse attitudes, often sub-liminally, which are hard to eradicate until they are exposed for what they are. For example, in preparing the original version of this text in 1968 'he' was used throughout without any thought as to the bias it proclaimed which was entirely cultural. The career woman was then largely unknown in industry outside certain functions such as personnel, medicine, and administration. Times have now changed and the career woman is the rule rather than the exception—though women are still poorly represented in senior management. The same is true of certain ethnic minorities—especially those we term 'coloured'. The individual charged with the task of recruitment is in the front line and needs to be very aware of 'unfair discrimination' and consciously seek to avoid it. Whilst I do not believe that one should exaggerate and whilst objective and factually based evaluations are acceptable, the question should be asked of all selection criteria; is this criterion socially just? Is this question or test unfairly loaded? Why do we think that a woman, an older man, an African national or someone with strong political views should be automatically excluded? The personnel department is the keeper of the organization's conscience in conforming to the law and in addition to this it should be responsible for recruiting the best people available. Many of these have been quite unfairly, and foolishly, rejected in the past for totally illogical and indefensible reasons such as sex, age, colour or creed.

A more subtle source of error is known as 'the halo effect'. This occurs when the interviewer, having been impressed favourably (or unfavourably) by one attribute of the candidate, allows any judgement of the candidate's other attributes to be swamped and assigns to them correspondingly high (or low) ratings. Thus an interviewer confronted, for example, by a candidate whose appearance and bearing seem to be ideal for that job may give her credit for more experience or intelligence than she really possesses. If most of the other applicants for the job have already been eliminated, the interviewer may be especially prone to this form of 'halo effect'.

*Note-taking*
Uncertainty about when, where and how to take notes during an interview seems to be a common source of difficulty to those with limited experience. Some note-taking is usually necessary, especially by the inexperienced interviewer. This is particularly true when several candidates are to be seen in sequence and the time between interviews is short.

The approach to note-taking must vary according to the interviewer's powers of concentration and the reliability of her or his memory. Both faculties can be cultivated to a high degree by systematic training, but the untrained memory is notoriously selective and fickle. The personnel officer must develop the ability to recall accurately what has been said during the past hour or so. This calls for no superhuman effort; it is a requirement of the job. Ability to do this is taken for granted in other spheres. All professional actors accept that they must memorize vast quantities of dialogue, actions and movements. Likewise, professional interviewers will minimize their dependence on written notes, and will need only a few 'prompts' to revive their memory of an interview. The following points are helpful as a practical guide:

(a) Always ask the candidate's permission before taking notes. Few refuse and, indeed, many seem pleased by the implication that what they are saying is important enough to be recorded.

(b) Never take notes furtively. Write quite openly, but in such a position that the candidate is unable to read what is written.

(c) Take a minimum of notes and confine them to 'memory triggers' and important facts not recorded elsewhere. They should serve as *aide-memoires* and not as a verbatim recording.

(d) Never let note-taking interrupt the flow of conversation.

(e) Be careful about timing. Highly personal or adverse information should not be noted until the conversation has moved to a different topic.

*Number of interviewers*

For the great bulk of recruitment work the one-to-one type of interview (ie one interviewer with one candidate) is most frequently used. Even so, the candidate will often have more than one interview before being offered an appointment, the preliminary screening being conducted by a member of the personnel department and the subsequent interview by the head of the department concerned. For certain types of appointment, there can be advantages in having more than one interviewer present but it must be remembered that this will produce a very different reaction in the mind of the candidate.

The one-to-one situation is generally preferred, because rapport is established more easily and it allows the interviewer to be more flexible in approach and in the framing and timing of follow-up questions. Candidates respond more naturally and freely in the informal atmosphere of this setting. It also makes less heavy demands on management time, since the second interviewer sees only those applicants who have survived the preliminary interview. Conversely, more of the candidate's time is taken up by a sequence of interviews and, if these cannot be held on the same day, there may be a risk that the most able applicant will be offered and accept a job elsewhere.

Some authorities recommend that two interviewers should see the candidate simultaneously and claim that this method reduces bias and subjectivity. Two interviewers can be useful in situations when a large number of applicants must be seen in a short period of time, and when one of the interviewers is a technical expert. Even so, it is important that the interviewers should have agreed beforehand the role which each is to play. Usually, one conducts the greater part of the interview, whilst the other observes and makes notes until being invited to pose specialist or supplementary questions towards the end of the discussion. This type of interview situation does, of course, have value in the training of new interviewers.

Panel interviews are favoured by some writers. The panel usually comprises three to five assessors. Its principal value in industry is at the final short list stage for some senior appointments, when several departments need to be identified with the eventual appointment. Advantages claimed for the panel interview are that it reduces bias and subjectivity; ensures that an expert on each topic asks the questions; enables user and other departments to be represented; increases impressiveness and formality; sets up uniform standards of judgement; and requires candidates to explain themselves only once. But, unless all the assessors are highly trained and adhere to their allotted roles, most of these potential advantages will be lost. In the governmental, educational or local authority ambience, where they are widely used, its weaknesses are that one interviewer with a strong personality can dominate the others; members of the panel may tend to show off to impress each other; formality reduces flexibility and inhibits the establishment of rapport; some candidates may be overawed or reluctant to talk freely on personal matters; only the formal behaviour of the candidate is observed; the smooth flow of conversation is obstructed and the pattern of questioning can become haphazard unless it is firmly controlled.

Selection boards comprising more than five assessors are rarely used as a serious selection device in industry. Insofar as they appear to exist, they are often little more than a convenient vehicle for introducing the final candidate(s) to a full committee; in many cases, the effective choice will already have been made by a sub-committee or by a permanent official whose recommendation is being submitted for ratification.

*Interpreting the interview*

By the end of the interview, the candidate and the interviewer will each have accumulated facts and impressions which they did not have before. Each is faced with the task of digesting and interpreting this new information. The interview is a two-way affair. Information flows in both directions and a separate assessment is made by each party. If the interview has been conducted properly the candidate will have a fairly detailed picture of the company, the job, co-workers, and the conditions of employment. Some of the more important gaps in his or her knowledge will have been filled in by observation and by asking questions during the course of the interview. Impressions will have been formed about the interviewer (who personifies the company for the candidate) and also about the way in which information has been given or withheld. On such evidence a decision will be made as to whether or not to accept the job if it were to be offered.

For her part, the interviewer will have learned much from the candidate's questions, as well as from her own. She will have noted the type and depth of the questions, the candidate's grasp of the information given to him, the quality of his reasoning and his verbal ability. These clues will be stored in the interviewer's mind, together with all the other evidence acquired during the selection process which she must now marshall and analyse. The framework she uses is the person specification (described in chapter 1). Throughout the interview she will have borne in mind the essential and desirable attributes demanded by the job and particularly any contra-indications which may have been specified. Her task now is to judge how closely the candidate meets those requirements.

In some cases, the interviewer will already have concluded on factual grounds that the candidate is unsuitable for the job by failing to meet one of the essential requirements. Even so, a fairly full assessment should be recorded so that the candidate may be considered in relation to other vacancies which could arise in the future. More often, the interviewer has to judge the degree to which the candidate possesses the desired attributes. This is done by considering all the clues picked up at various points throughout the interview. Evidence about the candidate's interests, for example, may have emerged when discussing family circumstances, school hobbies, attitude to overtime work etc, and the interviewer must piece this information together in order to discern the underlying pattern. One practical method of doing so is to:

● assemble the facts of the candidate's career in chronological order;
● superimpose the candidate's explanations and attitudes using quotations of the candidate's actual words when possible;
● examine the trends and behaviour patterns;
● consider the candidate's progress and rate of development in relation to peers. Compared with people from a similar background and with similar opportunities, has her/his progress been below average, about average or better than average?

Whilst the interview is in progress and afterwards, the interviewer will formulate working hypotheses about the candidate and then search for evidence in past and present behaviour to confirm or refute those hypotheses. A useful technique is to visualize the candidate at work in typical situations and to consider how she might behave. ("I can see her coping convincingly with even our toughest customers . . .").

The interviewer aims to build up a coherent picture of the salient features of the candidate's life. Only a few bare bones had previously been apparent from the candidate's own written statements. Flesh is added by piecing together all the further information gleaned from the interview. This process of reconstruction and appraisal is a vitally important one. By taking into account what the candidate has already achieved and why he has done so, the interviewer is better equipped to judge how that candidate would be likely to perform if faced with the demands inherent in the job for which he has applied.

*Information sessions*

A new technique which the author has been developing is that of a formal 'information session'. This can be group or individual and is especially appropriate at senior levels or when a project team is being assembled or where the competition is open, eg public appointments. Candidates are given a full brief beforehand and encouraged to do their own search about the company and its executive team. This may be supplemented by a formal audio/visual presentation at the short list stage at the beginning of the day. Candidates are then invited to ask questions and to make observations. In effect there is a reversal of roles with the candidate in charge of the seminar. This technique has been used in two ways:

(a) potential colleague—candidates for a board appointment have met other directors/departmental heads either as a group (preferably) or individually. Insight, judgement, tact, inter-personal sensitivity and management style are quickly revealed.

(b) potential superior—the candidates (individually) spend a set time (40 mins) with two to three future key subordinates seeking both information and to set a basis for a future working relationship. Quality of questioning and handling of the session are recorded by observers supplemented later on by comments from the 'interviewees'.

In both cases the seminars are timed and observed by trained observers with a written brief and ratings are made.

On the whole the reaction of candidates has been very favourable although the seminar, run in an informal atmosphere, is demanding—and revealing. The 'interviewees' must be carefully briefed not to take over the session and to keep to the point in their answers.

## iii   Group selection methods

Among the qualities which neither the interview nor intelligence tests are able to assess accurately are the candidate's ability to get on with and influence future colleagues, to display qualities of spontaneous leadership and to produce ideas in a real life situation. To meet this need, group selection procedures have been evolved. They usually take the form of a group exercise centred on a real or imaginary problem. Developed by the German army before the

1939–45 war, they have since been used extensively for officer selection in HM Forces, by the Civil Service Commission, and for assessment prior to management training courses by some industrial concerns. Given adequate safeguards they can be used with success also in the selection of executives.

Group procedures are not used as widely as might be expected for several reasons, perhaps the chief ones being the difficulty of recording and interpreting the information, the time taken and the unwillingness of some candidates to participate in a face to face competitive situation.

## *Purpose*

Group procedures are designed to provide evidence about candidates' abilities to:

● get on with others;
● influence others, and their manner of doing so;
● express themselves in verbal terms;
● think clearly and logically;
● argue from past experience and apply knowledge, intelligence and experience to a new problem.

They also reveal the type of role they tend to take in a social group.

These characteristics break down into two major parts: intellectual skills and social skills. In addition, other personality factors are displayed and these may substantiate impressions gained during the interview, such as the existence of strongly held attitudes, likes and dislikes.

## *Procedures*

Three main types of situation or exercise can be used. These are:

(a) Leaderless groups (usually discussion)
(b) Command or executive exercises
(c) Group problem-solving

## *(a) Leaderless groups*

About six to eight candidates are given a topic of general interest to discuss: or they may be asked to choose their topic. The setting has to be arranged carefully, so that no one chair dominates the rest. As with all groups, the members should be of reasonably comparable standing. The discussion is timed strictly, using a stop-watch, and everything is recorded and observed by a number of assessors placed inconspicuously in the corners of the room. The group do not know the topic for discussion until they have been briefed. ("We should like to hear your views on this topic. We want you all to take part, even if you feel you cannot contribute much to the discussion by way of experience: you may well have more experience to call on than you realize. You will have exactly . . . minutes. Tackle the subject in whatever way you feel to be most suitable. You may now start as soon as you are ready.")

Using a system of recording *who-said-what-to-whom*, the observers assess the type and quality of each member's contribution and the reaction of the others to it. At the end of the discussion, the group are thanked and given a break, while the assessors consider and compare their rankings.

The encouraging—and perhaps surprising—point about the leaderless discussion group, is that each member tends to play a similar role on each occasion, provided that the topic is a controversial one of general interest.

### (b) Command or executive situation

The candidates are given an extensive brief, based on a real life situation. In executive selection this might be the description and history of a company, including its leading personalities and current problems. The brief then leads to a typical job problem. The candidates are given the brief on the previous day, and have time to study it. Executive roles are allocated. On the following day, each in turn takes the chair, outlines a solution to one of the problems and defends it before the rest of the committee. Sometimes a composite problem is used, where each will take an extended role throughout the whole period.

Again, the members are observed throughout and rankings are compared.

### (c) Group problem-solving

This is a combination of the other two. The group is leaderless and is usually described as an advisory committee: how it organizes itself is left to the group to decide. The problem is often relevant to the job which is to be filled. It should be preferably beyond the experience of any individual in the group, but one to which each member can contribute according to knowledge, experience and intellectual skill. The problem is generally a large one, so that pressure is imposed to solve it within the given time.

Members of the group are carefully briefed and timed. As with other group selection methods, their behaviour is observed and recorded, but in assessing individual contributions previous experience is taken into account.

*Interpretation*
Social skills: Each candidate is ranked on social skill and the role taken (or attempted). Social skill includes sensitivity to others, tact, aggressiveness, hostility, friendliness, withdrawal, reaction when contradicted or criticized; how the candidate saves face or modifies his or her views. Social role takes account of the extent to which others listen to, ignore, shout down or become hostile to him or her; whether he/she becomes accepted as chairperson, expert, group coordinator, ideas person etc. The way the candidate attempts to influence others, the way others are handled and the amount of respect engendered will be the major things looked for.

Intellectual skills: The quality and quantity of the candidate's contributions are analysed for clarity of thought; ability to express ideas logically and forcibly; the quality of analogies and generalizations; ability to apply both knowledge and experience to the problem; flexibility of thinking and the weight carried in argument or discussion.

Principal ratings are generally given on account of general intelligence displayed; quality of argument; influence in argument; and ability in applying knowledge and experience.

Strong attitudes: These are often provoked in discussion but difficult to detect during an interview. The staunch authoritarian, the 'leaf in the wind', the fairminded, the 'one solution, one problem' people all come to the surface at some time or other. Strong political, racial or religious attitudes may often be revealed.

Self or 'buddy' ratings: After the discussion, candidates are sometimes asked to assess the contribution of the other members and to express their likes and dislikes of them. Sometimes they may be reluctant to do so, but generally this can be achieved, and sociograms compiled of the results.

*Difficulties implicit in group selection—when to use and when not to use:*
Group exercises are time-consuming and therefore costly. They are appropriate only for appointments where social leadership skills are required; hence they can be used for supervisory and management appointments and, at the final short list stage, can be a convenient means of seeing all the candidates on one day.

They are less likely to be successful when used with under 18s, and even then should be reserved for the A level group. The younger ones are unlikely to contribute much and, in any case, may not take the procedure sufficiently seriously. Their experience is limited and their ideas are still in the formative stage. Likewise group procedures are unlikely to be particularly successful with people who are not very articulate or who are not used to solving problems by the means of words. In theory it would of course be possible for a group of manual workers to solve a design problem by the use of hand and machine tools and materials. One would not normally need to test such ingenuity in this way. To aid the less articulate it is possible to produce a series of documents of a type with which they will be familiar so that they have the basic problem solving material in their hands. At one time, following the use of group selection and assessment procedures for the selection of officers during the war, they became a favourite tool with ex-service industrial managements for the selection of future management trainees. Hence they tend to be used for the selection of the more articulate school leavers, for graduates and for others who wanted to join management training courses. They have been used over the years by firms of consultants in the selection of senior management, but they are not a popular device among senior, experienced candidates from outside a company.

Today group selection procedures outside the civil service tend to be used much more for in-company selections to supervisory or to managerial posts. Although candidates are in direct competition they do know one another and there is a feeling that this is a much fairer way of selecting people. All are set the same task to perform and are judged on their work performance rather than, say, on their past record. Group selection procedures can be as successful in selecting future supervisors as in selecting future general management.

The assessment centre concept has been growing in popularity in the United States and this is extending to Europe: groups of employees are put through a series of tests and group exercises at an assessment centre, which is equipped to administer such tests and will train company personnel in the interpretation of test results.

Composition of the group is important and there should be about six to eight participants. They should all be of similar ages and have roughly the same level of experience. A mixed group of men and women is generally to be avoided except at more senior levels. Until society as a whole has accepted full equality among the sexes and until the individuals are sufficiently mature, male dominance or the tendency to impress the other sex will destroy the value of the session by uncontrollable distortion. Choice of topic is also important and should be decided by a psychologist or trained layperson.

A major drawback in using group selection techniques as part of a normal recruitment procedure, particularly with older and more experienced candidates, is that the identity of each candidate becomes known to the others. This can be a serious consideration when the field to choose from is small, or candidates are drawn from competing companies. The acceptability of the selection procedure can stand or fall by this criterion alone, which should always be carefully weighed in advance. Very broadly, group selection methods are acceptable to the under 40s, and to aspiring executives if the field of candidates is reasonably wide.

The personnel manager who may be contemplating using group exercises for the first time is advised to become thoroughly acquainted with the relevant literature. A course of training in the principles, and some practice in their interpretation, is highly desirable.

## iv   Psychological tests

Using selection tests is not a new idea. Examples can be found in ancient literature and throughout history[1]. However, the introduc-

[1]Two selection tests were used by Gideon in choosing 300 men from his army of 32,000 to fight the Philistines. See *Old Testament*, Judges VII, vv 1–7.

tion of psychological tests into industry has been fraught with suspicion and misunderstanding. Controversy persists in spite of abundant evidence that certain tests, properly used, have high predictive value in the occupational sphere. They are being employed on an increasing scale in the UK, but not as yet to the same extent as in the United States. Selectors and candidates are likely to feel strongly about tests; and a number of popular books have been published on the subject, in addition to the considerable scientific literature. Emotion can run so high that the value and limitations of tests fail to be seen in a true perspective. In recent years many tests have had to be very carefully pruned to ensure that they are genuinely 'culture fair' and eliminate social, racial or sexual bias. This is no mean task; some aspects can pose very serious technical problems to the test constructor especially if the test is to be applied to newcomers to a country or those brought up within exclusive communities within the host country.

Test scores should never be used as the sole criterion in making an appointment. Tests do not supplant the interview but, in appropriate cases, they can supplement and strengthen it. The interview has too many advantages to be discarded. Quite apart from its technical value as an assessment technique, it serves as a flexible and convenient framework for a face to face meeting and has the intrinsic merit of enabling questions about the job to be raised and answered. Tests can, however, measure some attributes which are difficult to assess by interview. They can thus help to reduce the areas of subjective judgement and of possible human error in the selection process as a whole. A word of warning is necessary: tests in the hands of an untrained person can be more misleading than helpful. That is not to say that only the qualified psychologist can make use of tests (though this does apply to some of them). However, the inexperienced person does need a formal course of training in how to apply and interpret those tests which are available for use. This chapter summarizes the main types of tests which are of potential interest to the practising personnel officer and indicates the circumstances in which they may be helpful. It also suggests that either a formal training course in psychological testing should be taken or the interviewer should refrain from dabbling with such tests.

*Main types of tests*
The tests in current use fall into five main categories, each of which
is briefly described below:
  (a) General intelligence (or general aptitude)
  (b) Special aptitude (loosely referred to as 'aptitude')
  (c) Attainment
  (d) Typical performance
  (e) Personality

*(a) General intelligence tests*
Intelligence is one of the hardest things to assess accurately from
interview evidence alone. Verbal fluency can easily be mistaken for
high intelligence and, conversely, hesitancy in speech may be
confused with low intelligence. The candidate with an indifferent
scholastic record may yet possess considerable innate ability which
was not fully tapped during school days. Tests of general
intelligence can help the personnel officer to recognize such cases.
Before describing intelligence tests, it is necessary to consider what
is actually meant by 'intelligence'.

Controversy persists in academic circles about the precise
definition of 'intelligence'. The subtleties of the arguments need
not concern us here, since most psychologists are broadly agreed
about what the term conveys. In lay language, intelligence tests are
simply a means of measuring performance on a standard series of
mental tasks; and they are important because it can be shown
statistically that a person's ability to score highly on such tasks
correlates with the capacity to learn and retain new knowledge, to
pass examinations and to succeed at work. The fact that a person
has the necessary mental capacity does not, by itself, guarantee
success at work; but if that capacity is lacking, success will never be
attained however hard he or she may try.

Vincent[1] postulates three forms of intelligence: *innate intelligence*, ie a person's capacity to perform on a standard series of mental
tasks; *effective intelligence*, ie the extent to which that capacity is
used in real life situations; and *practical intelligence*, ie worldly
wisdom or the ability to learn from experience and apply that
knowledge to new situations. Vincent suggests that "innate
intelligence and effective intelligence are closely related. Although

[1]Vincent, D F, *Age and Test Performance*, National Institute of Industrial Psychology,
Occasional Paper.

effective intelligence will vary with the occasion, persons of high innate intelligence will on average display high effective intelligence. The undoubted value of intelligence tests, that is, of measures of innate intelligence, is partly due to this relationship and partly to the fact that in the situations for which they are used to predict success, such as passing an examination or doing some responsible work, people usually do use their wits and their average effective intelligence is not usually lower than their innate intelligence. If the situation is one of importance, a person's effective intelligence is not likely to be much lower than the innate intelligence, but the efficiency with which the situation is handled, his/her practical intelligence, will depend upon innate intelligence plus knowledge plus experience."

Before using any test, the personnel officer must ensure that it measures accurately and reliably what it is supposed to measure. It must also be established that what the test measures is a significant factor in occupational success.

Most tests of general aptitude and of special aptitude contain a common factor (referred to as 'g') which is postulated as 'general intelligence'. This common factor is present to a greater degree in some tests than in others. A person with high general intelligence will do well, therefore, on all such tests, but performance may vary from one test to another according to the extent to which each test measures other special abilities as well. (The latter can be isolated or set in relief by tests of special aptitude.) Individual people are able to apply their general intelligence better to certain types of material than to others. Thus, some will respond best to verbal or language-based tests; others to a sequence of patterns and spatial designs; and others to tests based on numerical series. In order to arrive at an accurate measure of a person's general intelligence, it is necessary to use both a verbal test and a non-verbal one. The verbal (or v:ed) test reflects in known quantity a person's previous education; hence, when considered in relation to the amount of education already received, it may provide clues to ability to benefit further from verbally-based education or training.

*(b) Special aptitude tests*
Individual people differ greatly in their psychological make-up. Some possess a distinct flair for languages, for example, whilst

others are more at home with mechanical things. Tests have been devised to measure certain of these special aptitudes such as mechanical ability (including electrical and other engineering types of activity); clerical; numerical; spatial; and, to a lesser extent, artistic and creative capacities. These special aptitude tests are generally incorporated in test batteries, which also include tests of attainment and of general intelligence. As indicated above, a person with high general intelligence will score well on most of these tests depending on their 'g' content or loading. Special aptitudes can be discerned by comparing performance on the general and the special aptitude tests. Interpretive tables (or norms) have been devised on an occupational basis for some test batteries, thus enabling individual scores to be compared with these norms when selecting engineering apprentices, printing apprentices, trainee accountants, secretaries, computer program operators, clerical workers etc.

Manual dexterity is particularly hard to isolate, since it seems to take many different forms according to the degree of spatial judgement and coordination involved and the relative movements of the fingers, hands wrists and arms. No single test suffices for all permutations of manual dexterity, but many specific tests have been devised by psychologists to suit the particular demands of various jobs. These often take the form of timed runs on work samples. For semi-skilled jobs, quite a number of such tests have been devised and shown to be successful.

*(c) Tests of attainment*

Attainment tests seek to measure a person's range and depth of knowledge of a subject and grasp of its basic principles. Since the marking of such tests involves no subjective interpretation, they provide an accurate guide to a person's current knowledge and highlight strengths and weaknesses within that subject. With some job applicants, they can be a better indicator of current knowledge than school examination results, particularly if those examinations were taken some years ago; or if the candidate has a good short term memory without a proper grasp of the basic principles; or if the particular questions in the examination papers called on only a small sample of knowledge.

Although the unqualified can devise attainment tests they are ill-advised to do so, unless they have a thorough understanding of the statistical concepts involved. For example, a battery of attainment tests for secretarial work will cover vocabulary, grammar, spelling, punctuation, arithmetic etc, and within each aspect the items will be graded in order of difficulty, so that the battery will show the candidate's level of attainment and degree of accuracy.

### (d) Test of typical performance

This category of test is self-explanatory. Examples are shorthand and typing tests, with the items well graded in order of difficulty.

### (e) Personality tests

Originally designed as diagnostic aids to clinical and psychiatric medicine, several different types of personality test have been used successfully by members of the medical profession for many years. When transplanted to the industrial scene, personality tests become the most controversial of all psychological tests. Of course it would be tremendously helpful in industrial selection work if the interview evidence could always be supported by personality tests, of proven validity and reliability, which were acceptable in the normal course of assessing candidates. Unfortunately, that stage has not yet been reached. Much research is still needed. Some recent tests show promise but need considerable skill in interpretation. The personnel officer who is contemplating using any personality tests would be prudent to obtain professional advice before doing so; and the serious reservations held by many leading psychologists should be borne in mind. Many other types of test have been developed and tried, some with commercial success, based on astrology, colour preferences, a study of bodily movements and postures, palmistry, phrenology, graphology etc. Some undoubtedly are used extensively and their users claim to achieve commendable results and to gain valuable insights. There can be a positive correlation sometimes between the results of some of these and with 'standard' tests administered at the same time to the same people. Unfortunately, with these, objective measurement is often difficult to achieve. Thus, they are not respectable, academically or scientifically, and are mistrusted by the statistician. Research has been conducted over many years into biological phenomena (such as electro-chemical pulses, reactions and wave patterns) with interesting results, but these are still in their early days, and much more research needs to be done before they become commercially available.

### When to use tests

Since tests, like the interview, are a means of eliciting information about the candidate, much depends on what the personnel officer already knows about him or her and what it is necessary to find out or to confirm. The older the candidate, the more should be apparent already from the 'track record', provided that a good application form is being used. Hence, the marginal value of tests diminishes with age and, as a general guide, tests are not usually given to candidates over 40, except in special circumstances.

Acceptability is an important consideration. Tests can be made much more acceptable than is sometimes supposed, provided they are introduced carefully and explained properly. Grammar school and university leavers will take them without demur; aspiring executives under 30 will appreciate their relevance; ageing workers, transferring to other jobs, will accept them as inevitable; some executives over 40 may react unfavourably since the threat is greater, especially for successful people who have worked their way up from the bottom; and for executives over 50 tests are rarely of great value, since the peak of development will have been reached and practical intelligence is more relevant.

The appropriateness of testing will therefore vary according to the type and level of the various jobs to be filled. It is desirable for a company to give clear policy guidance on the range of jobs, if any, for which tests should be used as part of the standard selection procedures. In this way, the company will be able to compile its own test norms over a period, in relation to those categories of jobs. A number of test agencies and consultancies have been established which use specially validated test batteries which they have developed for specific clients and which are regularly applied and researched. Some large organizations have this as an internal service. Companies, or departments, refer individuals to them for an 'in depth' assessment, usually at the short list stage or when they want to promote from within. Other individuals can be referred to these and other psychologists for assessment against their management or functional norms which are often tentative, and therefore unpublished, but which nevertheless have a potentially high predictive value.

Tests can be particularly useful when:

Recruiting school leavers: The factual information obtainable from tests is especially valuable when selecting for apprenticeships and for other long courses of training. Some firms give general intelligence tests to all school leavers, and special aptitude batteries to the more promising ones. When interpreted in conjunction with a professional vocational guidance interview, tests can assist remarkably in launching school leavers on a suitable vocation at the right level.

Assessing 'trainability': With more mature applicants, too, tests can be helpful in selecting those most likely to respond to training. A battery of general intelligence, special aptitude and attainment tests is most commonly used to measure capacity and 'trainability'.

Assessing for promotion or transfer: Not all good skilled workers have the capacity to become good supervisors, nor all sales representatives to become sales managers. Nor for that matter do good line managers necessarily make good general managers. On promotion other skills will be needed; in many cases skills analysis has shown that frequently new managers have to learn virtually entirely new jobs, since for 75 per cent or more of their time they will need to use an entirely new range of skills. Rosemary Stewart and her team at the Oxford Centre for Mangement Studies have done some interesting work in this area. Research experiments have shown a positive correlation between intelligence (especially verbal intelligence) and managerial potential. Given an employee's academic and career record plus a measure of innate capacity, a reasonably accurate prediction can be made of ceiling for promotion. Similarly, when considering the possible transfer of an ageing skilled worker to office work, a clerical battery can indicate whether the employee's abilities lie in that direction.

A further situation is where major change is to be introduced following, for example, a change in management style or mode of working as a result of a takeover or merger. Tests can remove a lot of the guesswork and provide objective, unbiased evaluations and reveal ability to respond to retraining and adapt to change or fit into a new cultural structure.

*How to use tests*
It is essential to adhere strictly to the testing conditions laid down in the manual supplied with the tests. Applicants must be introduced to the test situation with extreme care. If the selector explains why the tests are being used, suspicion will be allayed and resistance will diminish. Tests should be given when the candidates are mentally fresh and they should therefore form an early part of the selection procedure.

Many tests have an initial practice section, which is not scored, to ensure that all candidates are familiar with what is expected of them. They also serve another purpose. Coaching in test methods, like coaching in school examination methods, can enhance an individual's performance marginally. Doing similar tests several times can also produce a marginal improvement. The practice sections serve to reduce these effects. Some publishers supply parallel tests of equivalent difficulty as a means of overcoming the effects of coaching and practice.

Test scores are usually interpreted by referring to tables of norms. These enable the candidate's performance to be compared with the known performances of hundreds, and sometimes thousands, of other people of similar age and education. Thus each candidate can be ranked in relation to a much larger population than lies within the personal experience of the assessor. Validity researches showing correlations between test performance and later academic or occupational success are also available, so it is possible to assess the statistical probability of the candidate reaching the required level of attainment. On some types of test (but not all) there is a predictable decline in performance as age increases, and age adjustment tables are supplied.

In recruitment work there are three distinct stages in interpreting the candidate's test performance in order to predict suitability:
(i) actual scores are related to the appropriate norms tables;
(ii) test performance is compared with career record;
(iii) the latter are related to the requirements of the job.

There are divided views on whether the test results should be made available to the interviewer before or after seeing the candidate. Some interviewers feel that they might be over influenced by knowing the test results in advance; and others feel that the test results help them to pitch the interview at the right level and to seek explanations for apparent inconsistencies. There is no absolute rule. Much depends on the style and professional competence of the interviewer.

## v  Points of reference

It is common practice for an offer of appointment to be made "subject to satisfactory references". This escape clause is often inserted even though the employer may not bother to take up references or may consider it unnecessary to do so. It is easy to fall into the trap of regarding references as a procedural appendage which comes after the effective decision to engage an applicant has already been made. This attitude of mind can cause the selector to overlook sources of information which may be very important indeed. Properly conceived, references are an integral part of the assessment process.

Towards the latter stage of the selection process, the assessor has learnt a good deal about the candidate. But inevitably that knowledge is based on only a small sample of the candidate's total experience and behaviour. Moreover, much of it has been derived in the formalized contexts of application forms, psychological tests, interviews etc. These contexts are not, and cannot be, typical of the conditions under which the candidate normally works or will be required to work if engaged. Before reaching a final assessment the personnel officer must ask how much of this information consists of established facts about the candidate and how much is made up of impressions and unsubstantiated claims. From this a decision must be made on what else is needed to find out or confirm. Some of these gaps in knowledge can be filled by seeking 'references', in the widest sense of that term.

It is true that a reference usually cannot, and should not, be obtained from the candidate's present employer, until an offer of engagement is being made; even then, no approach should be made unless and until the candidate's explicit agreement has been obtained. But that is only one source of relevant information. Other sources are available and can be used without risk of embarrassment to the candidate.

*(a) School record*
When assessing school leavers or juveniles already employed, confirmation of scholastic achievements can be obtained from the headmaster or youth employment officer. Head teachers can often predict fairly accurately students' chances of passing academic examinations for which they are still studying, and for examinations where academic standards are known such as a university degree. Some employers are prone to assume that head teachers can also predict a student's suitability to join their company. Clearly, it is unreasonable to expect this, unless the employer has first taken the trouble to give a clear understanding of the particular type of job or apprenticeship for which the girl or boy is being considered. Heads and careers teachers will also give you useful comparative data such as how well a pupil mixes at school, interest in out of curriculum activities, and the amount of leadership displayed and responsibility taken while at school. It is not then difficult to translate this type of information to the industrial or commercial environment. On the whole the reports of handicrafts or art teachers are rarely useful, as standards set at school are so far below those expected in industry. Indeed, I have known a so-called prowess of young people in such subjects as geometrical drawing at school to bear an inverse relationship to their later skill on the drawing board.

*(b) Professional qualifications and university degrees*
Confirmation is readily obtainable. A printed form or model letter is a useful and acceptable method of requesting this confirmation. It should always show the candidate's full name and the exact dates on which the relevant examinations are claimed to have been passed.

Many professional bodies publish year books which list the names of their members. Reference to up to date year books can save time, when large scale recruitment of professionally qualified staff is being undertaken. They need to be interpreted with care, since the absence of the candidate's name may be due to nothing more sinister than a printer's omission or the fact that a subscription has lapsed.

### (c) Open testimonials

No hard and fast rules about written testimonials can be laid down. Much depends upon what is said and who says it. Some firms prefer to give testimonials to employees who are leaving, in order to save the time that might otherwise be taken up in answering subsequent requests for references from prospective employers. If testimonials are couched in factual and explicit terms, they should not be dismissed out of hand. Many are openly addressed "To whom it may concern", precisely because the employer is well-satisfied with an employee's work and wants to show that this is the case. Even so, they are often too generalized to be of much value. For example:

> *This is to certify that John Brown is an honest and conscientious worker. During his period of employment here, he has been given a variety of jobs to do and has tackled them to the utmost of his ability. We wish him well in his future career.*

Not surprisingly, this type of testimonial (often produced during the course of an interview) is read solemnly, and then quietly disregarded. It conveys virtually nothing of value. On the other hand, the example below *(if true!)* would convey a good deal of worthwhile information about the same person:

> *I hereby certify that John Brown has been employed at this garage since 1981. He is a thoroughly reliable and conscientious mechanic. In the course of his work here, he has undertaken major overhauls and minor repairs on many different types of cars, motor cycles and lorries, including diesel-engined vehicles. Although he did not serve an apprenticeship, he can be relied upon to carry out repair and maintenance work to a high standard, and without supervision. He gets on well with customers and workmates, and has always shown himself to be a man of sober and temperate habits. We are sorry that he has decided to leave us but recognize that we cannot offer him the early advancement which he merits.*

### (d) Closed references

Other people's assessments of the candidate's character or employment history can be taken into account more systematically by asking them for references. Their value will depend on how well the referee knows the candidate and on the exact wording of the questions asked. A reference is a privileged document, and that privilege must not be abused; all statements must be true or honestly believed to be true by their author. The more factual the reference, the easier it is to substantiate, the easier it is to convey and the easier it is to interpret. Employers are more willing than is sometimes supposed to supply confidential and factual answers to questions about a former employee's length of service, duties, rate of pay, reasons for leaving etc.

The method of obtaining references will vary according to the type and level of the job to be filled. Generally, it is not desirable to ask for names of referees to be submitted on the application form. To do so may make some potential candidates apprehensive, even if coupled with a statement that the referees will not be approached unless permission is granted at a later stage. It is usually better for the assessor to request the names of two or three referees towards the close of the interview, by which stage the particular points on which further evidence is needed will have been identified, and the employer can ask for referees who are in a position to supply it.

The questions put to referees need to be framed clearly and precisely. It is prudent to prepare a set of model letters so that an appropriate one can be modified, if necessary, to suit the particular circumstances before being sent to the referee. With weekly-paid operatives and clerical staff, the questions will mostly be designed to yield factual confirmation about a candidate's previous job. Especially revealing can be a final direct question such as "Would you re-engage her for that type of work?" With more senior appointments the referee's views may be sought, additionally, on the candidate's strengths and weaknesses in relation to the job applied for, which presupposes telling the referee about the critical demands inherent in that job. In such cases, an explanatory letter to the referee arranging to telephone her or him can be a useful technique. It assures the previous employer of the *bona fides* of the caller and gives an opportunity to check facts and refresh his or her memory about the candidate; and it also enables the prospective employer to take into account the manner in which the referee answers preliminary questions and to follow up, whenever necessary, with more rigorous supplementary questions.

Little reference has so far been made in this book to the

practice of executive search or headhunting, largely because much of what has already been said is equally appropriate whether the method used is executive search or advertising or by getting one's employees to introduce possible candidates. One significant variation however is in the checking out of candidates. The executive searcher, who by definition is working in a field where there are no more than, say, a maximum of 200 possible candidates, seeks to find out the reputation of each of those people by market research. This will be done by means of 'desk' search by 'using contacts'. At the desk search stage directories will be studied, as well as professional lists, professional and technical journals, national newspapers and relevant management magazines, These will all indicate who is and is not in the news, which particular companies are doing well and which are doing badly. Using a network of contacts the reputation of people is then checked. Then it is necessary to find who precisely is responsible for a company's good or bad results and who is a rising or declining star. It follows that most of this is done without the candidate's knowledge and therefore extremely discreetly. When the executive searcher has managed to narrow the list down to say 10 to 15 people they will be interviewed, so that a personal impression can be formed and the job can be 'sold' to them. Subsequently a candidate may be asked to give further referees, which may include such people as suppliers or customers or sub-contractors. But here of course the candidate is given every opportunity to contact referees in advance so that the background to the conversation may be known.

# 4
# Fourth stage—placement and follow-up

## i Final assessment and placement

Towards the end of the selection process, a wealth of information about the candidate will have been gleaned from correspondence, application form, interviews and, possibly, from tests and group selection procedures. Many applicants, perhaps the majority, will have been eliminated at one or other of these hurdles. A few may have withdrawn, either because some aspect of the job holds less attraction for them than they had at first hoped or because they have accepted a different job elsewhere. The personnel manager's next important task is to reach a final assessment of each surviving candidate. This must be done in order to arrive at a positive decision or recommendation on which, if any, of them should be offered an appointment. This is done by referring again to the person specification.

In practice, constant reference will have been made to this yardstick throughout the earlier stages of the selection process. At this stage it is used to piece together all that has been learnt about each individual. Two complementary aspects are involved. Firstly, an item by item comparison of the candidate's attributes with each specific requirement of the person specification. Many interviewers find it helpful to adopt a grading scale to quantify their impressions during or immediately after the interview. A five-point scale (A, B, C, D, E) is commonly used. If finer discrimination is needed, this can be converted into a nine-point scale as follows: A, B+; B, C+; C, D+; D, E+; E. Each attribute is rated separately and is also summarized in narrative style. It is safer to use alphabetical rather than numerical gradings. With numerals it is a temptation to add up the marks awarded under each heading in order to arrive at a total assessment. This can be misleading. The separate requirements rarely, if ever, carry equal weightings. Obviously, a candidate with inadequate experience for the job should finish up with a low overall assessment even though the physical appearance may be admirable. The final assessment, therefore, cannot be simply an arithmetical average or total of the separate items. It has to be a synthesis reached after weighing all the candidates' strong and weak points. The item by item analysis should ensure that no vital point has been overlooked; but we can only employ 'the whole person', not a bundle of qualities. The second aspect therefore is a separate and final appraisal of the 'candidate as a whole' in the light of all the available evidence. This, too, can be expressed as a grade and should always be accompanied by a descriptive summary of that candidate's significant strengths and weaknesses.

A systematic method of recording assessments will facilitate the subsequent task of making comparative judgements about the respective merits of those candidates who match the person specification most closely. There is no simple formula for doing this. If one candidate stands out head and shoulders above the rest in all respects, there is no problem. More often, there may be several candidates whose overall ratings are fairly similar. The ratings themselves cannot be accepted a having absolute accuracy and consistency, since the selector's standards may have shifted slightly during the interviewing programme. The selector will be better able to differentiate between them, if each key requirement of the person specification is reconsidered and the candidates are ranked in order of merit in relation to each requirement, after having first reviewed all the relevant evidence about them. At this stage it should be possible to decide which candidate should be offered that job.

This process sounds complicated. It is; but people are complicated and it will never be a simple task to assess them fairly. In some recruitment situations, less elaborate methods have to be used, but the basic principles should still be followed. When, for example, a large number of unskilled employees has to be engaged, the personnel manager may have to concentrate on ensuring that the immediate candidate meets the person specification; and, if labour is needed urgently, a decision to engage that candidate until everybody else has been interviewed cannot be deferred, however desirable that may be in theory.

Alternatively, certain applicants may be worth considering for one of several different vacancies, in which case they must be mentally assessed against the differing demands of those jobs before a positive decision or recommendation about their engagement and placement is made. If they are equally suited to two jobs, both should be described to them and their preference taken into account.

The interviewer should ensure that a candidate does not accept a job without a clear understanding of all its conditions. The onus is on the interviewer to fulfil the second objective of the interview—to provide the candidate with an accurate picture of the job. In addition to verbal information, it is advisable wherever possible to give a more vivid picture of the job and working conditions by enabling the candidate to see it for her/himself. A visit to the department concerned is a normal routine in the final selection and placement procedure of many companies, and is usually made the occasion for meeting or having an interview with the supervisor.

During the interview, a decision may have to be made about the wage or salary which is to be offered to the successful candidate. Money may not always be as decisive a factor as many people believe, but it is a profoundly important part of the contract of employment. In industry two different codes of practice often exist side by side; one for the wage earner and the other for the salary earner. The wage earner will expect to be told the rate for the job at once. It is advisable to have all the relevant information prepared in writing, giving details of basic rate, overtime rates, merit increments (if any), piecework guarantees, special allowances etc. There is no room for manoeuvre if, as is often the case, these figures are governed by an agreement with a trade union. With salary earners, things are usually quite different. The candidate should have gleaned from the advertisement a good idea of the salary level of the job. The employer has probably obtained a reasonably good indication of the candidate's present salary from the application form, but may be uncertain of the candidate's expectations. It is up to the employer to broach this subject and to explain the probable starting salary, the basis of salary reviews, fringe benefits and any assistance that may be offered to meet removal expenses. A precise and irrevocable figure need not necessarily be quoted during the interview; but it is desirable to establish that the approximate figure which the employer has in mind is reasonably likely to be accepted by the candidate. At the interview stage, there may still be room for negotiation and adjustment by both parties. When a firm offer has been committed to writing, there is less flexibility and neither party may be disposed to modify its position.

## Contract of Employment

Not only is it statutorily obligatory, but it is basic good management practice to ensure that the new employee is fully aware of the exact nature of duties to be performed but also the terms and conditions under which they should be carried out. Where this is not straightforward (particularly regarding managerial appointments) it is a good plan to have a further meeting before the contract is finally drawn up to discuss it in detail with the prospective employee. Many companies, aware of the burdensome impact of high taxation, are prepared to be more flexible over salary/fringe benefit than before. A candidate with a private car but high mortgage may prefer cash towards running the car rather than a company car; some may prefer a higher pension benefit than cash and so on. At this stage also the actual job description should be given to the new person and if necessary modified so as to remove any doubts. Far too often, in the author's experience, people join companies expecting one thing and discovering another on arrival. This is not deliberate (we trust!) but due to a lack of proper communications. If the proposed organization structure won't work, far better to sort it out in advance with the new employee than expect to resolve it when he or she has to sustain the full pressure of the job.

Contracts should be clear but not rigid. If the job is going to develop and change as the new employee progresses, make reference to it. A key task job description is less likely to give rise to dispute than a detailed list of duties; the latter is sure to omit some and can provide a field day for the politically motivated union official.

Besides details of hours of work, salary and benefits, job title, to whom one is responsible and where the work is located, the grievance procedure must be stated. In the past, many of these were contained in a booklet which was handed to the new employee, who was advised to read it and to sign a form to say this had been done. It is sensible to spell out the details (eg the company pension scheme) in a booklet but the critical points must be set out in the contract and the employer must make sure that the prospective employee understands that before joining. It is therefore usual to send a copy in advance and to run over the detail in the first morning if not before. A contract of employment, since the Contract of Employment Act (1972) and the Employment Protection (Consolidation) Act (1978), is now far more legally binding than before and both parties need to be absolutely clear as to what is agreed: for the employer, failure to do so can be very costly indeed.

What of the candidate who is eliminated? It should be borne in mind that the third objective of the interview is so to conduct it that whether the candidate is engaged or not he or she feels fair treatment has been given (see page 116). If he or she does not meet the requirements of any of the available vacancies, an effort should be made to help the candidate accept the fact. Very often it is possible to do this by pointing out those requirements of the job which are not within his or her power to meet. If this is tactfully done the candidate should be able to appreciate the wisdom of the decision. There are occasions, however, particularly where qualities of personality are involved, when it may not be possible to tell the candidate precisely why their application has been rejected. In such cases, emphasis should be placed on the useful qualities the candidate possesses, and some advice given on the type of work in which these qualities could be used.

## ii  Induction

The responsibility of the recruiter does not end when the person arrives for the first day's work. There is a period of after-care which is vitally important. Much of this can be carried out by the new employee's supervisor, but the personnel manager should ensure that it is done. He or she will have taken the first steps on receipt of the acceptance letter.

The personnel manager must try to see that the new person will be able to settle in quickly and that forseeable problems are dealt with in advance. People cannot work well if they are worrying about resettling their family or finding it difficult to raise a mortgage. A leaflet giving local information and guidance on such matters can be sent to new employees before they start.

There is a limit to the amount of new information which an

employee can assimilate on the first day. Everything is strange and new. Almost everyone is a stranger. The personnel manager should plan the induction programme with this in mind. Some administrative matters have to be dealt with immediately and it is sensible to have a standard checklist of these so that nothing is overlooked. The employing department can generally be made responsible for introducing the new starter to immediate colleagues and indicating the cloakroom, canteen etc. It is as well to make sure that even these obvious aspects are not left to chance. The personnel manager will usually explain welfare and personnel services as part of the induction process. The new employee can be reminded of the function of the personnel department and encouraged to raise any settling-in problems so that these can be nipped in the bud before they develop into serious difficulties. It is advisable to visit each new starter at the place of work during the first few days. This need not take more than a couple of minutes but is the best way of making sure that all is going well.

New employees want to prove their worth as soon as possible after their arrival. The more quickly they are helped to find their feet, the better will be their impression of the company they have joined.

## iii Follow-up of results

At this point the most crucial stage of selection work has not even started yet. Nor could it have been.

The whole purpose of recruiting is to find people who will prove to be well matched to the jobs for which they are engaged. It is certainly not to produce a succession of new starters. Knowledge of results is essential. The personnel manager cannot know whether the new employee's performance is satisfactory unless there is a systematic feedback of information about the employee's progress. This concept of feedback is most important, if high standards of attainment are to be reached in any field of human endeavour. The efficacy of selection work must be judged by its actual results.

Neglect of follow-up can have serious consequences. A poor selector may remain undetected for a long time and a considerable amount of money may be wasted through unnecessarily high labour turnover, or in training the wrong people. Furthermore, however sound the selection methods may be, some mistakes will occur, and when they do they should be remedied as soon as possible.

Like the preceding stages of the selection procedure, the follow-up must be systematic. An initial check should be made not later than one month after the date of engagement. The employee's supervisor or head of department should be asked to report the performance of the newcomer, basing that assessment on the requirements of the original job/person specifications. If the report indicates that the employee is not settling in well, the personnel manager must ascertain the reason. After discussion with the supervisor, it may be decided to provide additional training, to offer the employee a transfer to a different job or to await the outcome of a further follow-up. Whether the report shows a satisfactory performance or not, the employee should be told frankly at a private interview with the supervisor how he or she is progressing.

A single follow-up can seldom provide a sound basis for judging whether an employee has been suitably placed. A careful report after the first month may be adequate in the case of certain simple routine jobs. But when the work is complex, as in the case of executive appointments, or where there is a prolonged period of training, as in apprenticeships, a series of reports at regular intervals will be necessary. In companies that already operate a system of periodic assessment of all employees—whether this be done primarily for salary reviews, merit awards, training, promotion potential etc—information of value to the selector can be an additional by-product. If no such reporting system exists, the selector must institute follow-up procedures.

Whenever the results of a follow-up are at a variance with the selector's original assessment of an employee, the selection records should be carefully scrutinized for possible clues. This is made easier if comparable rating scales are used to record both the interview and the follow-up. If evidence is found that the selector repeatedly misjudges a particular attribute, he or she will know that extra attention must be paid to the methods of evaluating that attribute in future. Correlation of selection predictions with the candidate's subsequent performance is a necessary step towards the development of better selection procedures and greater skill in matching candidates and jobs.

## iv  Recruitment administration

Efficient recruitment includes a good deal of longer term preparation. The recruiter's task is facilitated if potential candidates can be predisposed to think they would like to work for the company. They are more likely to apply if they already regard the firm as a good employer. A good reputation has to be earned over the years. It can be consolidated or undermined by the way in which recruitment is conducted. Therefore the personnel manager must be sensitive to the climate of public opinion and must be concerned with the company's reputation or image as an employer. There is much that the personnel manager can contribute in that respect.

Over a period, attitudes can be influenced by the content and style of recruitment advertisements, particularly by those appearing in local newspapers which are used frequently. The advertisements can be regarded as an information channel through which to stimulate interest in developments taking place within the company and to convey something of its character, as well as serving the immediate purpose of publicizing specific jobs.

The planned release to the local newspapers of advance information on newsworthy developments is also a practical method of paving the way for recruitment, especially if it heralds a major expansion; and personnel managers should therefore keep in close touch with their editorial staffs. In fact, they should make it their business to know personally all those who are regularly concerned, directly or indirectly, with recruitment in that locality. This will include, for example, the manager of the local branch of the Department of Employment, youth employment officers, head teachers and careers teachers etc. Links with technical colleges may lead to requests for the company's products or processes to be included in displays or demonstrations. Representation on regional planning committees, participation in local exhibitions and occasional factory visits can all have some bearing on the long term task of building and sustaining the company's reputation. With forethought, much can be done that will facilitate the future engagement of the right calibre of employees at the time when they are needed.

Recruitment policy and procedures can and should be summarized in the form of a reference manual, the appropriate sections of which are held by each member of the staff who has a part to play. Whilst emphasizing the personal and confidential nature of recruitment, it should contain guidance on practical aspects such as the role of the recruiter *vis-à-vis* the line manager; standing instructions to gate-keepers, receptionists and telephonists; rules governing the reimbursement of travel expenses; personnel records to be completed; the use of model letters or printed reply slips; maximum time lapse permitted in dealing with applications; procedures for taking up references etc. It is neither possible nor desirable to legislate for every contingency, and room must always be left for the application of common sense. The manual must be reviewed periodically to ensure that administrative practices remain consistent with the basic policy intentions.

Applicants' early impressions of a company are influenced by the stationery and recruitment forms adopted. These should be well designed with simple and clear headings. Model letters to cover frequently recurring situations can be used to save both dictation and transcription time. They should be modified, as appropriate, to meet individual circumstances; and care must be taken lest specific questions asked by the candidate are ignored.

Printed acknowledgement slips and standard letters can help to ensure that each applicant receives a prompt reply and can save a good deal of staff time when confronted with a large number of applications. Carefully worded, they can be acceptable in some situations but, since they lack the personal touch, procedures regulating their use should be drawn up carefully.

Courteous reception depends on having suitably trained people as gate-keepers and receptionists. Signposts pointing the way to the personnel office should be installed on large sites. The waiting room need not be elaborately furnished, but it should be well lit and kept tidy. A mirror should be provided and there should be access to nearby lavatories. A table with writing materials will be needed for the completion of application forms and there must be a sufficient number of upright and reclining chairs. Up to date reading matter should be at hand and this may include literature about the company and its products as well as newspapers and periodicals. One member of the staff should be made explicitly responsible for seeing that the waiting room is maintained in good order at all times. Old magazines and burned out electric light bulbs present a poor impression of the company's standard of efficiency. Attention to detail and unfailing courtesy are the marks of the good administrator and imply that the company is genuinely interested in people.

*Summary of typical procedures*

To sum up, a typical recruitment programme might comprise at least a score of separate actions carried out in the sequence below. Each one is important. Mistakes often arise because insufficient attention is devoted to the earlier steps in the recruitment process.

1 Receive employee requisition (on standard form) from department manager.
2 Search files for the relevant job/person specification or for a similar one.
3 Discuss vacancy with supervisor, ensure that replacement is absolutely necessary, and arrange to interview present incumbent to explore reasons for leaving.
4 Review and modify job/person specification in the light of changes which may have taken place and agree these with supervisor and department manager.
5 Consider feasibility of internal promotion or transfer; failing which, determine the most probable sources of candidates and the most economical method of attracting them. Check whether any enquiries have been received from suitably qualified people in recent months.
6 Inform Department of Employment, employment agencies and/or prepare draft advertisement and select the most appropriate advertising media.
7 On receipt of applications, classify provisionally into (a) most likely, (b) possible, (c) unsuitable. Write or telephone promptly to (a) arranging interview if time is short and ask for completed application form to be returned with confirmation; send 'model' letter to (b) with application form; eliminate (c) unless suitable for alternative vacancy.
8 Acknowledge receipt of application froms and scrutinize for additional candidates who merit interview.

9    Conduct preliminary interviews, and use other assessment techniques as appropriate. (Note any candidate's travelling expenses.)

10   Compile shortlist, agree arrangements for final selection procedure with department manager.

11   Invite shortlisted candidates and arrange overnight accommodation if needed. Write to other interviewed candidates advising them that they have been unsuccessful.

12   Send copy of timetable to all staff affected, reserve interviewing rooms, order coffee, inform receptionist etc.

13   Conduct final assessment programme.

14   Prepare letter of appointment for successful candidate and agree arrangements for verifying qualifications, taking up references and attending medical examination with the candidate.

15   On confirmation of acceptance, write to unsuccessful candidates (and to any others who have not been turned down). In appropriate cases advise them that they will be considered for any suitable future vacancies which may arise.

16   Write 'starting instructions' letter to successful candidate.

17   Make out personnel records for new employee and inform department, accounts office etc of proposed starting date.

18   See that induction procedures are carried out.

19   Preliminary follow-up within one month to resolve any settling-in difficulties.

20   Subsequent follow-up and comparison of progress report with original selection assessment and predictions.

*Final Note*

The follow-up reports will produce some disappointments. No selector can expect to be proved right in every assessment ever made. They can be expected, however, to search relentlessly for ways of avoiding those mistakes and cannot be forgiven if they go on repeating them; the costs are too great. Recruitment and selection work must be carried out competently and conscientiously or a trail of industrial inefficiency and unhappiness may follow in its wake. Those engaged in this work, whether regularly or occasionally, must always be mindful of the personal responsibilities they carry. People make companies. And the selector chooses those people. But recruitment and selection work is not carried out in a vacuum and its results cannot be judged as though it were. It forms only one part of personnel management, albeit a most important part; and as with any other branch of personnel work its full benefits will accrue only where the company's personnel policy as a whole is sound.

# Selected Bibliography

## Recruitment

ADVISORY, CONCILIATION AND ARBITRATION SERVICE. *Recruitment and selection*. London, ACAS, 1983. (Advisory booklet 6)

ATKINSON John. *Recruitment after the recession*. Falmer, Institute of Manpower Studies, 1982. (Report 43)

BAIRD Robert B. *The executive grapevine*. 4th ed. London, Executive Grapevine, 1985.

BRAITHWAITE Roderick *and* SCHOFIELD Philip. *How to recruit*. London, British Institute of Management, 1979

COURTIS John. *The IPM guide to cost effective recruitment*. 2nd ed. London, Institute of Personnel Mangement, 1985

EUROSURVEY LIMITED. *Management recruitment: the ways and means*. Rev. ed. London, Eurosurvey, 1983

FINNIGAN John. *The right people in the right jobs*. 2nd ed. Aldershot, Gower, 1983

HACKETT Penny, SCHOFIELD Philip *and* ARMSTRONG Michael. *The Daily Telegraph recruitment handbook*. 2nd ed. London, New Opportunity Press, 1982

HUBBARD G. "The recruitment jungle". *Management Today*. September 1984. pp 84–86, 88

INSTITUTE OF PERSONNEL MANAGEMENT. *The IPM recruitment code*. 3rd ed. London, IPM, 1983

INSTITUTE OF PERSONNEL MANAGEMENT. *Legislation for personnel managers: a check list*. London, IPM, 1982

INSTITUTE OF PERSONNEL MANAGEMENT *and* BRITISH INSTITUTE OF MANAGEMENT. *Selecting managers: how British industry recruits.* London, IPM/BIM, 1980. (IPM information report 34; BIM management survey report 49)

JACKSON Matthew. *Recruiting, interviewing and selecting: a manual for line managers.* London, McGraw-Hill, 1972

LEICESTER C. "Recruitment in the 80s". *Personnel Management.* Vol 10, No 4, April 1978. pp 28–31

MANGUM S L. "Recruitment and job search: the recruitment tactics of employers". *Personnel Administrator.* Vol 27, No 6, June 1982. pp 96, 99–102, 104

NEWELL David. *Understanding recruitment law.* London, Waterlow, 1984

PEARSON Richard *and* WALSH Kenneth. *How to analyse your local labour market.* Aldershot, Gower, 1983. (Institute of Manpower Studies series 2)

PLUMBLEY Philip *and* WILLIAMS Roger. *The person for the job: the complete guide to succesful recruitment and selection.* 2nd ed. London, Kogan Page, 1981

"Recruiting with the rules". *Employment Digest.* No 149, January 9, 1984. pp 1, 8

*Recruitment and selection.* Bicester, CCH Editions, 1985. (Personnel management in practice 1)

REES R. "Setting the scene for effective recruitment". *Works Management.* Vol 32, No 5, 1979. pp 114–16, 119

STOOPS R. "Managing recruitment costs". *Personnel Journal.* Vol 62, No 8, August 1983. pp 612, 615

UNGERSON Bernard, *ed. Recruitment handbook.* 3rd ed. Aldershot, Gower, 1983

WALSH Kenneth *and* PEARSON Richard. *UK labour market guide.* Aldershot, Gower, 1984. (Institute of Manpower Studies series 5)

WANOUS John P. *Organizational entry: recruitment, selection and socialization of newcomers.* Reading, Mass., Addison-Wesley, 1980

## Job Analysis

ASH R A *and* LEVINE E L. "A framework for evaluating job analysis methods". *Personnel.* Vol 57, No 6, November/December 1980. pp 53–59

BEMIS Stephen E, BELENKY Ann Holt *and* SODER Dee Ann. *Job analysis: an effective management tool.* Washington, D.C., Bureau of National Affairs, 1983

BOYDELL T H. *A guide to job analysis.* London, British Association for Commercial and Industrial Education, 1973

McCORMICK Ernest J. *Job analysis: methods and applications.* New York, American Management Association, 1979

MARKOWITZ J. "Four methods of job analysis". *Training and Development Journal.* Vol 35, No 9, September 1981. pp 112–15, 117–18

ROFF H E *and* WATSON T E. *Job analysis.* London, Institute of Personnel Management, 1961

ROULEAN E J *and* KRAIN B F. "Using job analysis to design selection procedures". *Public Personnel Management.* Vol 4, No 5, September/October 1975. pp 300–04

YOUNGMAN Michael Brendon *and others.* *Analysing jobs.* Farnborough, Gower/Teakfield, 1978

## Job Descriptions

Austin D L. "A new approach to position descriptions". *Personnel Journal.* Vol 56, No 7, July 1977. pp 354–55, 363, 365–66

Berenson Conrad *and* Ruhnke Henry O. Job descriptions: how to write and use them. Costa Mesa, Calif., *Personnel Journal*, 1976

Jones M A. "Job descriptions made easy". *Personnel Journal.* Vol 63, No 5, May 1984, pp 31–4

Klinger D E. "When the traditional job description is not enough". *Personnel Journal.* Vol 58, No 4, April 1979. pp 243–48

Ungerson Bernard. *How to write a job description.* London, Institute of Personnel Management, 1983

Webb Sue. "Preparing and using job descriptions". *Employment Bulletin.* Vol 1, No 8, November 1984. pp 58–61

## Recruitment Methods

Bucalo J P. "Good advertising can be more effective than other recruiting tools". *Personnel Administrator.* Vol 28, No 11, November 1983. pp 73–9

Cowton C J. "To advertise or to use a recruitment bureau". *Mangement Decision.* Vol 21, No 6, 1983. pp 31–8

"Headhunting: how the executive search game is played". *Personnel Executive.* Vol 1, No 3, September 1981. pp 28–31

Hoare D. "Helping the headhunter get his man". *Management Today.* November 1984. pp 41, 45, 48

Lubliner M J. "Developing recruitment literature that pays off". *Personnel Administrator.* Vol 26, No 2, February 1981. pp 51–4, 95

RAY Maurice. *Recruitment advertising: a means of communication.* London, Institute of Personnel Management, 1980

RUGMAN N. "Rooting out recruits: headhunting versus standard search". *Personnel Management.* Vol 11, No 6, June 1979. pp 42–4

SCHOFIELD Philip. "Getting the best from recruitment agencies". *Personnel Management.* Vol 13, No 8, August 1981. pp 40–3

## Selection

BERGER L A. "Beneath the tip of the iceberg". *Personnel.* September/October 1977. pp 61–67

GILL Deirdre. "How British industry selects its managers". *Personnel Management.* Vol 12, No 9, September 1980. pp 49–52

HOLDSWORTH R. "Selection tips for small firm managers". *Personnel Management.* Vol 7, No 3, March 1975. pp 31–3

INSTITUTE OF PERSONNEL MANAGEMENT. JOINT STANDING COMMITTEE ON DISCRIMINATION. *Towards fairer selection: a code for non-discrimination.* London, IPM, 1978

JEFFERY R. "Taking the guesswork out of selection". *Personnel Management.* Vol 9, No 10, October 1977. pp 40–2

LEWIS C. "Whats new in . . . selection". *Personnel Management.* Vol 16, No 1, January 1984. pp 14–6

MACKENZIE-DAVEY D *and* HARRIS Marjorie, *eds. Judging people: a guide to orthodox and unorthodox methods of assessment.* London, McGraw-Hill, 1983

MEYER John L *and* DONAHO Melvin W. *Get the right person for the job: managing interviews and selecting employees.* Englewood Cliffs, N.J., Prentice Hall, 1979

OWENS D *and* HARROWVEN L. "How to cope with a flood of job applications". *Perspective*. January 1982. pp 4–5

## Application Forms

DYER Barbara. *Personnel systems and records*. 3rd ed. London, Gower, 1979

KEENAN T. "Where application forms mislead". *Personnel Management*. Vol 15, No 2, February 1983. pp 40–3

PENDLEBURY C. "Application form design". *Industrial and Commercial Training*. Vol 2, No 11, November 1970. pp 527–29

## Selection Interviewing

ANSTEY Edgar. *An introduction to selection interviewing*. London, HMSO, 1977

ARVEY R D *and* CAMPION J E. "The employment interview: a summary and review of recent research". *Personnel Psychology*. Vol 35, No 2, Summer 1982. pp 281–322

AUSTIN D L. "Interviewing candidates for managerial positions". *Personnel Journal*. Vol 62, No 3, March 1983. pp 192–94

BAYNE R. "Can selection interviewing be improved?". *Journal of Occupational Psychology*. Vol 50, No 3, 1977. pp 161–67

BOLTON G M. *Interviewing for selection decisions*. Windsor, NFER-Nelson, 1983

*Croner's guide to interviews*. New Malden, Croner Publications, 1985

FRASER John Munro. *Employment interviewing*. 5th ed. London, Macdonald and Evans, 1978

GOODALE James G. *The fine art of interviewing*. Englewood Cliffs, N.J., Prentice Hall, 1982

GOODWORTH Clive T. *Effective interviewing for employment selection*. London, Business Books, 1979

GREEN J. "Structured sequence interviewing". *Personnel Executive*. Vol 2, No 10, April 1983. pp 26–7, 29

GRUMMIT Janis. *A guide to interviewing skills*. London, Industrial Society, 1980.

HACKETT Penny. *Interview skills training: practice packs for trainers*. Rev. ed. London, Institute of Personnel Management, 1981

HIGHAM M. *The ABC of interviewing*. London, Institute of Personnel Management, 1979

LOCK Harold F. *Interviewing for selection*. 4th ed. London, National Institute for Industrial Psychology, 1972. (NIIP paper 3)

MACKAY Ian. *A guide to asking questions*. London, British Association for Commercial and Industrial Education, 1980

MACKENZIE-DAVEY D *and* McDONNELL P. *How to interview*. London, British Institute of Management, 1975

PALMER Robin. "A sharper focus for the panel interview". *Personnel Management*. Vol 15, No 5, May 1983, pp 34–7

PURSELL E D, *and others*. "Structured interviewing: avoiding selection problems". *Personnel Journal*. Vol 59, No 11, November 1980. pp 907–12

READING T. "How interviews fail". *Management Today*. April 1977. pp 33, 36, 38, 42

RODGER Alec. *The seven-point plan*. 3rd ed. London, National Institute of Industrial Psychology, 1970. (NIIP paper 1)

SCHWEITZER N J *and* DEELY J. "Interviewing the disabled job applicant". *Personnel Journal*. Vol 61, No 3, March 1982. pp 205–09

SHOUKSMITH George. *Assessment through interviewing*. 2nd ed. Oxford, Pergamon Press, 1978

THARP C G. "A manager's guide to selection interviewing". *Personnel Journal*. Vol 62, No 8, August 1983. pp 636–39

WHITTAKER Peter. *Selection interviewing*. Rev. ed. London, Industrial Society, 1977. (Notes for managers 24)

## Group Selection

ANSTEY E. "The Civil Service administrative class: a follow-up of post-war entrants". *Occupational Psychology*. Vol 45, No 1, 1971. pp 27–43

ANSTEY E. "The Civil Service administrative class: extended interview selection procedure". *Occupational Psychology*. Vol 45, No 3/4, 1971. pp 199–208

ANSTEY E. "A 30 year follow-up of the CSSB procedure, with lessons for the future". *Journal of Occupational Psychology*. Vol 50, No 3, 1977. pp 149–59

BRUSH D H *and* SCHOENFELDT L F. "Identifying managerial potential: an alternative to assessment centres". *Personnel*. Vol 57, No 3, May/June 1980. pp 68–76

BYHAM William C. "Assessing employees without resorting to a centre". *Personnel Management*. October 1984, pp 56–7

CIVIL SERVICE COMMISSION. *Report of the committee on the selection procedure for the recruitment of administration trainees*. London, Civil Service Commission, 1979

COHEN S L. "Pre-packaged *vs* tailor made: the assessment centre debate". *Personnel Journal.* Vol 59, No 12, December 1980. pp 989–91

FIELDS H. "The group interview test: its strength". *Public Personnel Review.* July 1950. pp 139–46

FINKLE Robert B. "Managerial assessment centres". pp 861–88 *in* DUNNETTE Marvin D, *ed. Handbook of industrial and organizational psychology.* Chicago, Rand McNally, 1976

FRASER J M. "An experiment with group methods in the selection of trainees for senior management positions". *Occupational Psychology.* Vol 20, No 2, April 1946. pp 63–7

HIGHAM M H. "Some recent work with group selection techniques". *Occupational Psychology.* Vol 26, No 3, July 1952. pp 169–75

JAFFEE Cabot L. *Effective management selection: the analysis of behaviour by simulation techniques.* Reading, Mass., Addison-Wesley, 1971

JAFFEE Cabot L. *and* FRANK Frederic D. *Interviews conducted at assessment centres: a guide for training managers.* Dubuque, Iowa, Kendall/Hunt Publishing, 1976

KEIL E C. *Assessment centers: a guide for human resource management.* Reading, Mass., Addison-Wesley, 1981

KNOWLES M C. "Group assessment in staff selection". *Personnel Practice Bulletin.* June 1983. pp 6–16

MACRAE Angus. *Group selection procedures.* 2nd ed. Windsor, NFER Publishing, 1970 (NIIP paper 5)

*The Method II system of selection (for the administrative class of the Home Civil Service): report of the Committee of Inquiry, 1969.* London, HMSO, 1969

MORRIS Ben S. "Officer selection in the British Army, 1942–1945". *Occupational Psychology.* Vol 23, No 4, October 1949. pp 219–34 *and* Vol 24, No 1, January 1950. pp 54–61

MOSES Joseph L *and* BYHAM William C, *eds. Applying the assessment centre method.* New York, Pergamon, 1977

STEWART Andrew. *The identification of management potential: a brief description and review.* Falmer, Institute of Manpower Studies, 1973

STEWART Andrew. *A way to find new managers.* Falmer, Institute of Manpower Studies, 1981

STEWART Andrew *and* STEWART Valerie. *Tomorrow's managers today: the identification of management potential.* 2nd ed. London, Institute of Personnel Management, 1981. (Management in perspective)

THORNTON George C *and* BYHAM William C. *Assessment centres and managerial performance.* London, Academic Press, 1982. (Organizational and occupational psychology)

UNGERSON Bernard. "Assessment centres: a review of research findings". *Personnel Review.* Vol 3, No 3, Summer 1974. pp 4–13

VERNON Philip E. "The validation of Civil Service Selection Board procedures". *Occupational Psychology.* Vol 24, No 2, April 1950. pp 75–95

VERNON Philip E *and* PARRY John B. *Personnel selection in the British Forces.* London, University of London Press, 1949

## Testing

AIKEN Lewis R. *Psychological testing and assessment.* 4th ed. Boston, Mass., Allyn and Bacon, 1982

ANASTASI Anne. *Psychological testing*. 5th ed. London, Collier-Macmillan, 1982

BARTRAM D *and* BAYLISS R. "Automated testing: past, present and future". *Journal of Occupational Psychology*. Vol 57, No 3, 1984. pp 221–31

BOLTON G M. *Testing in selection decisions*. Windsor, NFER-Nelson, 1983

CRONBACH Lee Joseph. *Essentials of psychological testing*. 4th ed. New York, Harper and Row, 1984

DULEWICZ V. "Uses and abuses of selection tests". *Personnel Management*. Vol 16, No 1, January 1984. pp 46–7

GUION Robert M. "Recruiting, selection and job placement". pp 777–828 *in* DUNNETTE Marvin D, *ed*. *Handbook of industrial and organizational psychology*. Chicago, Rand McNally, 1976

HACKETT Penny. "Personnel testing". pp 23–46 *in* ARMSTRONG Michael, *ed*. *Personnel and training yearbook and directory 1981*. London, Kogan Page, 1981

HOLDSWORTH R F. *Personnel selection testing: a guide for managers*. London, British Institute of Management, 1972

JESSUP Gilbert *and* JESSUP Helen. *Selection and assessment at work*. London, Methuen, 1975. (Essential psychology)

PEARN Michael A. *The fair use of selection tests*. Windsor, NFER Publishing, n.d.

SNEATH Frank, THAKUR Manub *and* MEDJUCK Bruce. *Testing people at work*. London, Institute of Personnel Management, 1976. (Information report 24)

STEWART Andrew M *and* STEWART Valerie. *Tests in personnel selection: the use of psychological tests in industry*. (Uxbridge, Brunel University, Institute of Organizational and Social Studies), n.d.

TYLER Leona E *and* WALSH W Bruce. *Tests and measurements.* 3rd ed. Englewood Cliffs, N.J., Prentice-Hall, 1979

"Using selection tests in recruitment and promotion". *Industrial Relations Review and Report.* No 177, June 1978. pp 2–9

VERNON Philip E. *Intelligence testing 1928–1978: what next?* Edinburgh, Scottish Council for Research in Education, 1979

## References

LEVINE Edward L *and* RUDOLPH Stephen M. *Reference checking for personnel selection: the state of the art.* Ohio, American Society for Personnel Administration, 1978

"References: a safety net, but they're no substitute for good judgement". *Perspective.* August 1983, p 5

## Induction

ADVISORY, CONCILIATION AND ARBITRATION SERVICE. *Induction of new employees.* London, ACAS, (1982). (Advisory booklet 7)

"Company induction programmes". *Industrial Relations Review and Report.* No 173, April 1978. pp 2–5

FOWLER Alan E. *Getting off to a good start: successful employee induction.* London, Institute of Personnel Management, 1983

INDUSTRIAL SOCIETY. *Induction.* London, Industrial Society, 1973. (Notes for managers 21)

MARKS Winifred R. *Induction: acclimatizing people to work.* Rev. ed. London, Institute of Personnel Management, 1974

SHEA Gordon F. *The new employee: developing a productive human resource.* Reading, Mass., Addison-Wesley, 1981

ST JOHN W D. "The complete employee orientation program". *Personnel Journal.* Vol 58, No 5, May 1980, pp 373–78

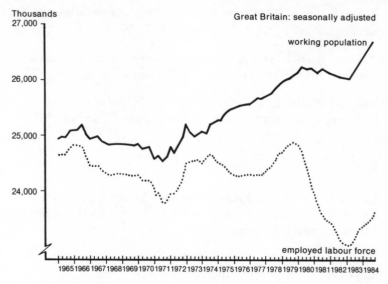

*Figure 1*
*Working population and employed labour force*

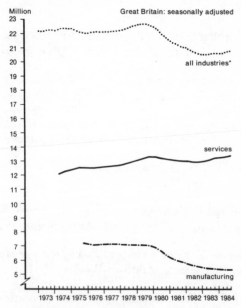

*Agriculture, energy, water supply and construction
**Source:** EMPLOYMENT GAZETTE HISTORICAL SUPPLEMENT No 1 *April 1985*

*Figure 2*
*Employees in employment by industry*

*Persons aged 16–59\* by economic activity, highest qualification and sex, Great Britain 1981*

| Highest qualification | Men | | | | | Women | | | | |
|---|---|---|---|---|---|---|---|---|---|---|
| | All men (000's) | Numbers of economically active (000's) | Economic activity rate/100 population | Numbers of unemployed (000's) | Unemployment rate/100 economically active | All women (000's) | Numbers of economically active (000's) | Economic activity rate/100 population | Numbers of unemployed (000's) | Unemployment rate/100 economically active |
| First or higher degree | 930 | 883 | 94.9 | 29 | 3.3 | 461 | 345 | 74.8 | 25 | 7.2 |
| Member of professional institution | 465 | 458 | 98.4 | 12 | 2.6 | 84 | 65 | 78.1 | 1 | 2.2 |
| HNC or HND | 361 | 350 | 97.0 | 11 | 3.1 | 48 | 39 | 80.7 | 1 | 3.8 |
| Teaching qualification | 116 | 112 | 96.7 | 2 | 2.2 | 424 | 314 | 74.0 | 13 | 4.1 |
| Nursing qualification | 44 | 43 | 97.9 | 1 | 3.3 | 539 | 410 | 76.1 | 16 | 4.0 |
| Trade apprenticeship | 3,272 | 3,195 | 97.6 | 244 | 7.6 | 453 | 288 | 63.5 | 26 | 8.9 |
| Trade apprenticeship not completed | 568 | 551 | 97.2 | 35 | 6.4 | 80 | 61 | 75.8 | 5 | 8.4 |
| ONC, OND or City & Guilds | 493 | 471 | 95.5 | 29 | 6.1 | 265 | 192 | 72.3 | 14 | 7.5 |
| 'A' level | 764 | 601 | 78.7 | 44 | 7.3 | 772 | 472 | 61.1 | 42 | 8.8 |
| 'O' level or equivalent | 1,387 | 1,133 | 81.7 | 109 | 9.6 | 2,476 | 1,648 | 66.6 | 140 | 8.5 |
| CSE (below grade 1) | 484 | 442 | 91.5 | 74 | 16.8 | 846 | 592 | 69.9 | 88 | 14.8 |
| Other | 467 | 444 | 95.1 | 43 | 9.7 | 734 | 501 | 68.3 | 34 | 6.8 |
| Still studying† | 363 | 92 | 25.4 | 33 | 36.1 | 365 | 81 | 22.3 | 27 | 33.1 |
| None | 5,623 | 5,128 | 91.2 | 732 | 14.3 | 7,743 | 4,471 | 57.7 | 444 | 9.9 |
| Not known or not stated | 574 | 461 | 80.4 | 34 | 7.3 | 519 | 275 | 53.0 | 20 | 7.4 |
| **All qualifications** | **15,910** | **14,365** | **90.3** | **1,435** | **10.0** | **15,810** | **9,753** | **61.7** | **896** | **9.2** |

*\*Includes some persons aged 60 born in January to May 1921*
†Includes full and part-time study
Source: Labour Force Survey 1981 (Series LFS No 3) HMSO 1982

*Figure 3. The qualified candidate market*

Economic status of persons aged 16 and over, analysed by age, sex and, for women, marital status, 1983*

Great Britain
Percentages

| Economic Status | Age | | | | | | | |
|---|---|---|---|---|---|---|---|---|
| | All aged 16 and over | 16–19 | 20–24 | 25–34 | 35–49 | 50–59 | 60–64 | 65 and over |
| **All persons** | | | | | | | | |
| *Persons (thousands) = 100%* | 42,334 | 3,531 | 4,141 | 7,442 | 10,036 | 6,117 | 3,126 | 7,941 |
| Economically active | 61 | 67 | 80 | 77 | 83 | 73 | 39 | 6 |
| Employed | 54 | 49 | 67 | 68 | 76 | 68 | 36 | 6 |
| Unemployed | 7 | 18 | 13 | 9 | 6 | 6 | 3 | 0 |
| Economically inactive | 39 | 33 | 20 | 23 | 17 | 27 | 61 | 94 |
| **All men** | | | | | | | | |
| *Men (thousands) = 100%* | 20,270 | 1,782 | 2,097 | 3,729 | 5,032 | 3,006 | 1,472 | 3,151 |
| Economically active | 76 | 69 | 90 | 96 | 96 | 89 | 60 | 9 |
| Employed | 67 | 49 | 73 | 85 | 88 | 81 | 53 | 8 |
| Unemployed | 9 | 20 | 17 | 11 | 8 | 8 | 7 | 0 |
| Economically inactive | 24 | 31 | 10 | 4 | 4 | 11 | 40 | 91 |
| **All women** | | | | | | | | |
| *Women (thousands) = 100%* | 22,065 | 1,749 | 2,044 | 3,713 | 5,004 | 3,111 | 1,654 | 4,790 |
| Economically active | 48 | 64 | 70 | 57 | 69 | 58 | 21 | 4 |
| Employed | 43 | 48 | 61 | 51 | 64 | 55 | 21 | 4 |
| Unemployed | 5 | 16 | 9 | 7 | 5 | 3 | 1 | 0 |
| Economically inactive | 52 | 36 | 30 | 43 | 31 | 42 | 79 | 96 |
| **Married women** | | | | | | | | |
| *Married women (thousands) = 100%* | 13,684 | 122 | 925 | 2,968 | 4,281 | 2,460 | 1,128 | 1,801 |
| Economically active | 50 | 47 | 57 | 53 | 68 | 57 | 22 | 4 |
| Employed | 46 | 32 | 49 | 47 | 64 | 55 | 21 | 4 |
| Unemployed | 4 | 15 | 8 | 6 | 4 | 2 | 1 | 0 |
| Economically inactive | 50 | 53 | 43 | 47 | 32 | 43 | 78 | 96 |
| **Non-married women** | | | | | | | | |
| *Non-married women (thousands) = 100%* | 8,380 | 1,627 | 1,119 | 745 | 723 | 651 | 526 | 2,989 |
| Economically active | 44 | 66 | 81 | 76 | 74 | 60 | 20 | 3 |
| Employed | 37 | 49 | 70 | 66 | 65 | 54 | 20 | 3 |
| Unemployed | 7 | 16 | 11 | 10 | 9 | 6 | 1 | 0 |
| Economically inactive | 56 | 34 | 19 | 24 | 26 | 40 | 80 | 97 |

*See notes to tables on page 4
Source: Labour Force Survey 1983 OPCS Monitor LFS 84/. (OPCS 1984)

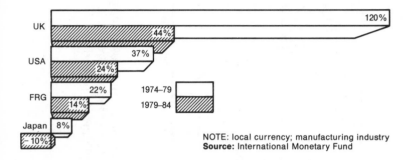

**Source:** EMPLOYMENT GAZETTE *April 1985*

*Figure 5*
*Rise in the unit labour costs 1974–1979 and 1979–1984*

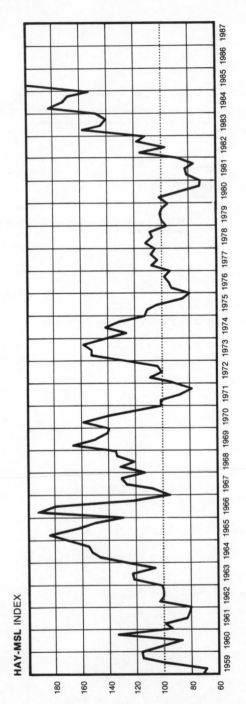

The above graph, which is derived from the HAY-MSL Index shows the number of managerial and senior appointments advertised in each Quarter, expressed as a percentage of the 1959 average. The HAY-MSL Index is based on a continuous analysis of all appointments advertised in seven national publications.

*Figure 6*
*Trends in the demand for executives*